DOO WOP MOTELS

—Kirk Hastings

Architectural Treasures of The Wildwoods

KIRK HASTINGS

STACKPOLE
BOOKS

Published by
STACKPOLE BOOKS
5067 Ritter Road
Mechanicsburg, PA 17055
www.stackpolebooks.com

Printed in China

10 9 8 7 6 5 4 3 2 1

FIRST EDITION

Design by Beth Oberholtzer
Cover design by Caroline Stover
Photos by the author unless otherwise noted

Cover: Caribbean Motel by David Harp, www.davidharpphotography.com
Frontispiece: Starlux Motel by Al Alven
Back cover: Admiral Motel by Al Alven, Caribbean Motel by Kyle Weaver, Starlux Motel by Al Alven, and Lollipop Motel sign by Kyle Weaver

Visit www.doowopusa.org for updates on all current Doo Wop happenings in The Wildwoods!

Library of Congress Cataloging-in-Publication Data

Hastings, Kirk.
    Doo wop motels : architectural treasures of the Wildwoods / Kirk Hastings.
    — 1st ed.
        p.   cm.
    Includes index.
    ISBN-13: 978-0-8117-3389-2 (pbk.)
    ISBN-10: 0-8117-3389-0 (pbk.)
    1. Motels—New Jersey—Wildwood—History.   2. Resort architecture—
New Jersey—Wildwood—History.   I. Title.

TX909.H27   2007
910.4609749'98—dc22

                                                                2006023142

CONTENTS

Hunt's Shore Theater, built in 1939, at Schellenger and Atlantic Avenues in Wildwood, in its August 1964 heyday. The building was designed in the Art Deco style prevalent at the time. Notice its spectacular neon signage.

David Williams Collection

Good Vibrations

I was extremely fortunate growing up. By the time I was out of elementary school, I had already seen many exotic, interesting places: Tahiti, Hawaii, Aruba, Waikiki, the Caribbean, Tangiers, Key West, Montego Bay, just to name a few. I was also privileged to have seen Monaco, the Acropolis, the Alps, Athens, Barcelona, the Coliseum, Madrid, the Mediterranean, Nantucket, Nassau, Quebec, and the Sahara. But in the process, I never left southern New Jersey.

How is that possible? you might ask.

I grew up in Wildwood Crest, New Jersey, one of four adjacent, similarly named towns on a small, seven-mile-long barrier island situated near the southern tip of the state. The other towns are Wildwood, North Wildwood, and West Wildwood, and collectively they all are known as The Wildwoods.

All of those foreign, romantic places that I saw were there, back in the 1960s when I was growing up. And many of them are still there today. They are imaginatively designed tourist motels.

Some of Wildwood's motels were built during the post–World War II decade of the 1950s, but most of them were built in the early to mid-1960s.

Later on, in the 1980s and 1990s, their unique building style became recognized throughout America, known as Googie architecture on the West Coast and eventually as Doo Wop on the East Coast.

But to me, growing up, they were just really interesting, unusual buildings, built during a decade of tremendous cultural creativity.

I left Wildwood Crest, and New Jersey, in 1969 but returned in 1973, spending the rest of the seventies and eighties there. During those decades, when there was a drive-in motel on practically every corner in The Wildwoods, I strolled on many a warm summer evening down Ocean Avenue, one block west of the Atlantic Ocean, where most of the Crest's motels were located. During the summer months, this avenue was always active and alive with the hustle and bustle of vacationing tourists and families enjoying themselves at the various motels. Cars featuring license plates from practically every state in the country were parked everywhere. Brightly illuminated neon signs lit up the night in a kaleidoscope of bright colors and futuristic designs. Even the air in the Crest's motel district possessed its own particular ambience—a combination of the distinctive smell of chlorine from the many motel swimming pools there and the fresh, salty ocean air.

The title page of a brochure advertising the Wildwoods by-the-Sea in 1966. David Williams Collection

The expansive beach of Wildwood Crest is almost a quarter mile wide, and because of tidal patterns, it continues to grow larger every year.

The world-famous Wildwood Boardwalk, as it appeared in the mid-1960s. David Williams Collection

A page from a 1966 brochure, extolling the virtues of Wildwood's world-famous Boardwalk.
David Williams Collection

The Boardwalk at Night — is a completely different world with hundreds of shops and many restaurants, snack bars and a large variety of games, a beautiful sight to see, all lit up. If you desire a little more excitement there are also four great amusement centers.

The world-famous flying ramp of the iconic Caribbean Motel, built by Lou Morey in 1958, at Buttercup Road and Ocean Avenue in Wildwood Crest.

A rear view of the Satellite Motel's cantilevered roof and pool area.

Up until the beginning of the twenty-first century, most of these buildings remained virtually intact, with few changes, appearing just as they had in the fifties and sixties. To natives who grew up in The Wildwoods and the countless visitors who have vacationed there over many summers, these buildings were all familiar friends. Somewhere along the line, they became frozen images from our collective childhoods that we never really gave much thought to over the years, because we assumed, perhaps naively, that they would always be there.

But now, in the early twenty-first century, it is becoming clear that these buildings, with their distinctive appearances and character, will not always be with us. Many are crumbling from old age as they enter their fifth decade of existence, and because of a real estate boom in The Wildwoods, others are being demolished at an alarming rate to make way for more modern—but very bland and boxy-looking—condominiums.

Now that these classic buildings are starting to disappear, people are beginning to realize just how significant—and architecturally important—they have always been. These structures are actually a lot more than just buildings. They are imagination run wild, with soaring ramps and crazy angles. They are visual wonders, with boomerang roofs, slanted walls, and kidney-shaped swimming pools. They are nostalgia, reminding us of a simpler, more optimistic time. And their plastic palm trees give us a sense of the exotic and tropical in a place that can get very cold in the wintertime.

Most of all, they are fun. Not many buildings are fun, but the ones that are remain etched in our memories long after they are gone. There is a magic there that is hard to explain.

The Wildwoods have always had a kind of magic in abundance. Despite real estate booms and economic fluctuations, I hope they will never completely lose it. But only time will tell.

CHAPTER 1

Don't Know Much about History

September 1, 1945: World War II was finally over. Thanks to the industrial shot in the arm created by the war and greatly increased production levels at home, America was primed for the greatest economic expansion in the history of the world. The sacrifices of the war years were over—the scrap, metal, rubber, and paper drives. A large production and industrial force was in place, and it no longer needed to focus on creating weapons and armaments for American troops. Now it could turn its attention to producing domestic goods for the returning GIs and their families.

And now that the GIs were finally home once again, their young families were beginning to grow—rapidly. In the 1970s, social scientists looked back on the postwar years and began to refer to the huge population increase between 1945 and 1963 as the baby boom generation. Retailers and service organizations at the time saw it as potentially the greatest consumer market the world had ever seen.

One product that began to be mass-produced almost immediately in the late 1940s was the automobile. Major manufacturers had severely halted production of new cars during the war years in order to conserve materials needed for the war effort. Now they returned to new-car production

Hotel Dayton, Wildwood and Atlantic Avenues, Wildwood-By-The-Sea, N. J.

with a vengeance. With more cars available, more people had cars to travel about the country in. As a result, the interstate road system was greatly expanded to meet this need, and American society became more mobile than it had ever been. That soon created another national market: the small roadside motel.

Previously, most traveler accommodations were higher-end hotels or more modest tourist courts, tourist camps, and boardinghouses. But by the 1950s, these places were becoming less popular with the new breed of traveler. Whereas single males traveling for business reasons had once been the major clientele of hotels, now more and more families—with new

Sherbrooke Family Apartments, built in 1959 on Farragut Road in Wildwood Crest's motel district. The structure resembles the classic Wildwood L-shaped motel more than it does an apartment building.

cars, kids, and plenty of disposable income—were traveling and taking vacations together. Fancy hotels were generally too expensive and inconvenient for them to stay in with children, and they wanted something better than the tourist camps and crowded boardinghouses. This led to the proliferation in the fifties of the motor hotel, or motel for short, a name first coined by the Milestone Motel way back in December 1925 in San Luis Obispo, California.

Early Motels in The Wildwoods

It was not long before the new-style motels began to pop up in The Wildwoods. Though fashionable Victorian-style hotels and boardinghouses such as the Manor, Lincoln, and Beachwood Hotels had been the accommodations of choice there for shore travelers during the first half of the twentieth century, beginning in the mid-1950s the new smaller, more modern-looking motels began to replace them. These two- and three-story mom-and-pop motels, generally owned and operated by married couples and individualistic in appearance, were less expensive to stay in and more informal. The motel usually had an outdoor pool for the kids and plenty of free parking for the family car, typically right in front of or beside the room. Thus there was no need to check in or out every time someone wanted to leave the premises. Plus with no clerks, no doormen, and no bellhops, no money had to be spent on tipping. All the guest had to do was step out of the motel room, jump into the family car conveniently parked right outside, and take off for fun and adventure—perfect for the more contemporary, on-the-go tourist.

The genesis of what would later become the modern tourist motel in The Wildwoods actually began back in 1939, when the Ship Ahoy was built by Ben Schlenzig at Taylor and Ocean Avenues. The Ship Ahoy was a rectangular, two-story, wood-frame building with thirteen small, one- and two-bedroom units. A balcony with a wooden railing that resembled the rail of a ship, complete with real life preservers, wrapped around the front and sides of the building. The Ship Ahoy was not really a hotel, because there was no restaurant or lobby in the building—only a small office on the first floor, the rear of which also doubled as living quarters for the owner-operators. Each unit had its own bathroom, and thus there were no communal areas in the entire building.

But the Ship Ahoy was not really a motel. It had no outdoor pool, was not L- or U-shaped, and had always been consistently listed in directo-

The Ship Ahoy, built in 1939, was one of the earliest motel-style structures in Wildwood, predating the later Doo Wop motel buildings of the 1950s and 1960s.

ries and telephone books under apartments. Two very similar motel-apartment buildings, the Sun Dial and Sun Deck, were built by Schlenzig at Andrew and Ocean Avenues in the 1940s. These were not strictly motels either. In the 1960s, the Ship Ahoy was moved from its original location and now stands at Washington and Baker Avenues in Wildwood, near City Hall. The Sun Dial and Sun Deck were also later moved to other locations.

Early postcard photo of Jay's Motel, the first motel in The Wildwoods, built during the winter of 1951–52 by Morey Brothers Builders on Atlantic Avenue in Wildwood.
David Williams Collection

The first building specifically referred to as a motel in The Wildwoods was the single-story Jay's Motel, located at Hildreth and Atlantic Avenues in Wildwood. The original owners, the Juvinos, contracted Will and Lou Morey (known at the time as Morey Brothers Builders) to construct the building during the winter of 1951–52.

The Morey Brothers

Lewis J. and Wilbert C. Morey were born under modest circumstances in tiny West Wildwood—Lou in 1925 and Will in 1927. After World War II, the two brothers built a number of single-family dwellings in The Wildwoods, and in 1950, they made their partnership legal with the formation of Morey Brothers Builders. Jay's Motel was their first motel project, but it was not typical of their later motel buildings. Inspired by winter vacations in Florida, the Morey brothers based Jay's on the style of many Florida motels of the period, with pink stucco outer walls and jalousie windows. It also featured an outdoor swimming pool and a separate building that did double duty as the motel's office and the owners' living quarters.

For whatever reason, the Morey brothers decided to dissolve their formal partnership on December 31, 1955. In early 1956, Will began construction of the Fantasy Motel at 131 West Rio Grande Avenue in Wildwood. At an overall cost of $125,000, a huge sum for the time, the Fantasy was advertised as being the "Newest Look" in motel design for The Wildwoods, and it certainly was that. It consisted of twenty-one units on two floors and was shaped like a large L, with a rectangular outdoor pool located in the elbow. All the rooms were connected to one

Will Morey Sr., working on a Doo Wop motel in Wildwood Crest in the early 1960s. Jack Morey Collection

another by an outdoor wraparound balcony decorated with rectangular panels that each had a lightning bolt design in the center. The color scheme of the motel was eye-catching, with bright yellow exterior walls and pastel sea green doors. But what really made the building unique was the southern section of the L, which faced Rio Grande Avenue. It was also two floors in height, with the motel office and summer living quarters for the owners, Will and his wife, Jacqueline, on the first floor. The second floor had a large, glassed-in playroom and lounge surrounded by an open-air sundeck. The lounge featured a gigantic, upswept roof design topped off by a large, ornate neon sign made by Allied Signs of Wildwood. The overall effect was completely new and modern, unlike anything seen before in the area.

    The Fantasy opened on April 29, 1956, and that date could be convincingly argued as being the beginning of the Doo Wop motel era in The Wildwoods. Though a few other motels had opened on the island since Jay's in 1952, such as the Flame Inn Motel in North Wildwood and the Wingate

The Fantasy Motel, built in 1956 by Will Morey on Rio Grande Avenue in Wildwood, was the motel that initiated the Doo Wop architectural style in The Wildwoods.

The sign for the Flame Inn, an early
motel in North Wildwood.
Kyle Weaver

Motel in Wildwood in 1953, the Fantasy represented a whole new concept in architecture that would start a building trend in The Wildwoods that would last well into the early 1970s. This trend was later referred to as mid-century modern or Doo Wop.

Will's new, futuristic-looking motel designs were inspired by similar buildings he had seen on winter vacation trips to Florida in the mid-1950s, particularly the motel structures built in Miami Beach and Fort Lauderdale by forward-thinking architect Morris Lapidus. Lapidus had studied architecture at Columbia University and was well established as a retail designer when he built his first hotel in 1954, the Fontainebleau, in Miami Beach. The Fontainebleau was different from anything that had been seen before. It was chock-full of imaginative, fanciful design elements such as cheese holes, round cutouts in the walls; woggles, free-form boomerang or amoeba shapes hanging from the ceilings; and exposed beanpoles, long, thin columns used as supports. Curved walls, columns ending in circles of light, and stairs that floated in space with no visible means of support

The Wildwood Diner, at Spencer and Atlantic Avenues in Wildwood, was built by the Superior Diner Company of Berlin, New Jersey, in 1955 and was expanded and enlarged in 1961. Constructed by one of Wildwood's mayors, it was later owned by another. Kyle Weaver

added to the building's modern-looking avant-garde ambience. Though many critics pooh-poohed it, the public loved it. The Fontainebleau was later used as a location for the 1960–62 ABC series *SurfSide 6* and the 1964 James Bond film *Goldfinger*.

The rest of the country also was being influenced by what was going on architecturally in Florida, as well as California. Diners, drive-ins, motels, coffee shops, and bowling alleys were becoming increasingly popular and widespread, many of them heavily influenced by the designs of Morris Lapidus and other, similar progressive-thinking California architects such as John Lautner of Googie's Coffee Shops, Stanley Clark Meston of McDonald's, Louis Armét and Eldon Davis of Denny's Coffee Shop, and Wayne McAllister of Bob's Big Boy Restaurants.

The Motel Battle in Wildwood Crest

By 1954, there were at least nineteen motels in Wildwood and North Wildwood. But early that same year, it was still illegal according to local zoning laws to build a motel in Wildwood Crest. Actually, the first building in the Crest with the word *motel* in its name had been the Eileen Motel at Lavender and Pacific Avenues in 1953, built by Francis R. McBrearty, but this modest structure more resembled a large bungalow with a couple of separate units incorporated into it than what would later be recognized as a full-fledged motor hotel. Residents insisted that they wanted the Crest to remain a bedroom community and not become a haven for the new large, commercial motel buildings that, in their opinion, were for "unmarried couples and wayward teenagers." But despite the objections of many residents, the Wildwood Crest commissioners approved an ordinance allowing limited motel construction in 1954.

The Breezy Corner Motel, located at Louisville and Seaview Avenues, was the second motel in the Crest. Built in 1954, it was a small, single-

Built in 1953, the Eileen Motel on Pacific Avenue was the first motel in Wildwood Crest, though architecturally it was more like a traditional bungalow court or apartment building.

The 1954 Breezy Corner Motel, on Seaview Avenue in Wildwood Crest, was one of the first motels to be built in the Crest. The rooftop sign's 1950s design is quite evident, but the neon tubing in the sign's lettering has been replaced by an exterior floodlight. Al Alven

story, L-shaped structure of ten adjacent units. But the battle over these newfangled motor hotels was heating up in the Crest. Despite more objections by residents—and the Wildwood Crest Civic Association—that year the town's commissioners approved ordinances allowing motel buildings to be built east of Atlantic Avenue along almost the entire length of the Crest. Their justification was that the Crest desperately needed the new commercial ratables in order to hold down the ever-increasing tax rate in the borough. The ordinances also called for Ocean Avenue in Wildwood, which was east of and ran parallel to Atlantic Avenue, to be eventually extended into the Crest to accommodate the new oceanfront motels.

Once legal restrictions were out of the way, the floodgates for new commercial development in the Crest were finally thrown wide open. During late 1955 and early 1956, the borough was inundated with applications for new motel construction. The small, eleven-unit Monta Cello Motel was built at Denver and Seaview Avenues in 1955. Located between Farragut and Stanton Roads, the Beach Waves Motel, a two-story, rectangular structure with a large parking lot and a separate coffee shop building, was the first beachfront motel to be built in the borough. During the spring of 1956, more local controversy was aroused when the owners, Erich and Anita Jung, petitioned the borough to build a forty-foot-long neon sign across the front of their new motel. Designed by the Ace Neon Sign Company of Wildwood, the sign would tower twenty-five feet in the air over the motel's front doors. Though some residents complained about the size of the sign, it was eventually approved, clearing the way for other, similar neon motel signs to be built in the Crest in the future.

The First Motel Boom Continues

At least partly because of the opening of the 200-mile-long Garden State Parkway in 1955, which made The Wildwoods much more accessible to car traffic, 1956 proved to be a banner year for motels on Five Mile Beach Island. Among others, the Sea Gull and Skylark Motels went up in Wildwood. The Packard Motel, consisting of fifteen units and named after the famous 1950s automobile, and the Sans Souci Motel, built by Will and Lou Morey and named after another famous Morris Lapidus hotel located in Fort Lauderdale, Florida, went up in North Wildwood. The Crest saw its share of motels rise, too, with the Vogue and Carousel Motels built a block apart on Lavender Road by Ralph and Earl Johnson, operating as Johnson

An early brochure rendering of the Sea Gull Motel, built in 1956, on Atlantic Avenue in Wildwood. Wildwood Historical Society

The sign for Skylark Motel. Kyle Weaver

Brothers Builders. The Vogue had only twelve units, but the thirty-unit Carousel was the largest motel yet to be built in the Crest.

On Thursday, May 24, 1956, a new restaurant opened in the Crest that was unlike anything that had ever been seen on the East Coast before, with the possible exception of Florida. Owned by William and Mary Schumann, Schumann's Restaurant, across the street from the Crest Pier Community Center on Atlantic Avenue, was designed and built by architectural innovator Will Morey, with a soaring prow-shaped roof, flagcrete stonework, and large sheet-glass windows that allowed diners an unobstructed view

This is what the Carousel Motel, on Ocean Avenue in Wildwood Crest, originally looked like when it was first built in 1956. Later its circular second-floor lounge was sacrificed for more room units. Wildwood Historical Society

The Carousel Motel, originally owned by its builders, Earl and Ralph Johnson, played host to many national celebrities in the 1950s and 1960s. Al Alven

Top: Schumann's Restaurant, built by Will Morey in 1956 on Atlantic Avenue in Wildwood Crest, right next to the Satellite Motel. Its prow-shaped roof resembles that of the Satellite. Chuck Schumann and David Williams Collection

Above: An early postcard view of the interior of Schumann's Restaurant, an excellent example of 1950s Coffee Shop Modern architecture. Chuck Schumann and David Williams Collection

Left: A late twentieth-century shot of the entrance to Schumann's Restaurant, showing the rooftop neon signage that was added later. MAC Collection

The front cover of the menu for Schumann's Restaurant from the 1960s. David Williams Collection

An example of flagcrete, a popular 1950s and 1960s siding used by many of Wildwood's motels. This sample is from the Jolly Roger Motel in Wildwood Crest, built in 1959.

of the neighborhood. Advertised as having a "California Atmosphere," referring to the famous ultra-modern 1950s California coffee shops designed by such farsighted architects as John Lautner and the team of Louis Armét and Eldon Davis, the eatery boasted high cantilevered ceilings, exposed ceiling beams, brightly colored geometric booths with Formica tabletops that seemed to simply hang suspended in space, sumptuous oak wall paneling, and light fixtures that looked like something out of a 1950s science-fiction movie.

In 1957, a number of other new motels went up in the Crest, such as the Bel Air Motel, named after another famous automobile of the time and shaped like the number 7, as well as the Coral Sands, Catalina, Conca D'or, Georgeanna, Sands, Town & Country, Silver Beach, and Markay Motels, all built by various local contractors, including Bada Brothers Builders and Buckingham Brothers Builders. But both Lou and Will Morey were quite busy in 1957 also. Between the two of them, they were responsible for the construction of the 24th Street Motel in North Wildwood; the Capri, Castaways, and Knoll's Resort Motels in Wildwood; and the Sea Chest Motel in

The Bel Air Motel, built in 1957, at Morning Glory Road and Ocean Avenue in Wildwood Crest, is a Doo Wop favorite with its angled roof and plastic palm trees.
Kyle Weaver

the Crest. But their most trendsetting motel of 1957 was the Ebb Tide Motel, at Heather and Atlantic Avenues in the Crest.

Lou Morey came up with the unique design for the structure for owners Harry and Margaret Stokes and Al and Agnes Beers. The Ebb Tide, named for the still popular 1953 song written by Carl Sigman and Robert Maxwell, was a three-story, L-shaped structure incorporating twenty-eight units and an apartment, plus a large sundeck on one section of the third level. All rooms were connected to each other by continuous outdoor balconies with wrought-iron railings. The motel's large office cubicle, added in 1958 and located at the west end of the L, was two stories tall and surrounded by large glass panels giving a striking see-through effect. The second level of the cubicle served as a combination lounge, TV room, and playroom.

But the most remarkable feature of the Ebb Tide was its leaning walls. Meant to suggest the ebb and flow of ocean tides, the bright yellow cement-based stucco walls (later repainted white) of the motel's first floor leaned inward at about a 65-degree angle, thanks to wood framing layered

The Bel Air Motel's tropical-looking pool area. Kyle Weaver

An old postcard shot of the famous Ebb Tide Motel, built in 1957 by Morey Brothers Builders at Heather Road and Atlantic Avenue in Wildwood Crest. The first Doo Wop motel in the Crest, it was featured in many national magazine and newspaper articles.

over top of concrete blocks. The walls of the second and third floors leaned outward, giving the building a distinctive look, as if it were about to collapse in on itself at any moment.

Will and Lou were on a roll now. During 1958, they were responsible for the Eden Roc Motel in Wildwood, named in tribute to the 1955 Morris Lapidus original in Miami Beach, as well as the El-Reno, Tangiers, and Swan Motels, all located in the Crest. Between 1956 and 1958, no fewer than 113 new motels had gone up in The Wildwoods. By the late 1950s, motels for the first time outnumbered hotels on the island.

The year 1958 saw two of the Morey Brothers' most exceptional motel projects to date completed. Will designed and built the Satellite Motel, which opened on May 17, at Aster Road and Atlantic Avenue in the Crest. Lou designed and built the Caribbean Motel a few blocks away, at Buttercup Road and Ocean Avenue. The Caribbean opened on June 6 of that same year.

The basic plan of the Satellite Motel, advertised as the "Motel of Tomorrow," was like many of the other motels being built in The Wildwoods, in that it was U-shaped, two and three stories tall, and featured a rectangular swimming pool in the center of the U. The east wing, which was three stories tall, consisted of eighteen units, all connected by external balconies with wrought-iron railings that incorporated interesting geometric shapes. The north wing was only two stories tall and consisted of seven units and

Close-up view of the Ebb Tide Motel in Wildwood Crest, showing its celebrated leaning walls. MAC Collection

The Eden Roc Motel, built by Lou Morey in 1958 on Atlantic Avenue in Wildwood, was named after the Morris Lapidus original in Miami Beach, Florida. Kyle Weaver

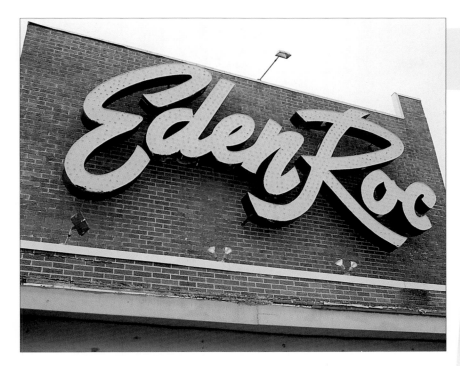

The huge, wall-mounted neon signage of Eden Roc Motel.
Kyle Weaver

East wing of the Eden Roc Motel, displaying its eye-catching Doo Wop design.
Kyle Weaver

The Tangiers Motel was built in 1958 by Lou Morey on Atlantic Avenue in Wildwood Crest. Despite its name, which evokes the city of Tangier in Morocco, northern Africa, the motel's design makes it look more as if it belongs in the South Pacific.

Smart and Luxurious

Swan
RESORT
MOTEL
WILDWOOD CREST, N. J.

An early postcard rendering of the Swan Motel. Wildwood Historical Society

an apartment that served as living quarters for the owners. But Will had by now learned how to make his motels look different from all the rest by employing Façadism, the particular use of a building's front façade to make a strong impression on passersby. The two-story western wing of the Satellite, on heavily traveled Atlantic Avenue, included a small office area on the first floor and a carport at the southern end. Above this was a much larger combination lounge and lobby, with huge plate-glass windows supported on the outside by a wooden latticework; inside was a curtain of hanging multicolored beads. A sundeck, supported over the carport by flagcrete columns, completed the southern end of this level. The immense asymmetrical cantilevered roof of the lounge and office resembled an enormous upside-down checkmark, recalling the distinctive roofs that architects Louis Armét and Eldon Davis had designed earlier that same year for the California-based Denny's Restaurant chain. The Satellite's angled roof looked quite similar to that of the next-door Schumann's Restaurant, also built by Will. Will obviously was now making a concerted effort to keep up with the newest trends across the country in modernistic architecture and include some of them in his building projects. The Satellite's effect was completed by a huge neon sign on the peak of the roof featuring various sputnik-shaped orbs and star shapes. Architectural expert and critic Thomas Hine, in his 1986 book, *Populuxe*, called the Satellite "a rather elaborate piece of space age folk art."

The Satellite Motel was built in 1958 by Will Morey on Atlantic Avenue in Wildwood Crest. Its boomerang roof design and early 1960s Space Age imagery identify it as one of Wildwood's most iconic mid-century Doo Wop motels. Al Alven

Will and his wife liked the Satellite so much that they moved out of the Fantasy Motel that summer and into the Satellite's living quarters, though they still maintained their permanent year-round home on Sweetbriar Road in the Crest.

The rooftop neon sign for the Satellite Motel, showing its Space Age imagery inspired by early 1960s space satellites. Kyle Weaver

A rear view of the Satellite Motel's angled roof and pool area.

Another view of the Satellite Motel, showing its eastern wing and room units.

Not to be outdone, Will's brother Lou went all out on his Caribbean Motel, built a few blocks away for Dominic and Julie Rossi. The Caribbean was originally linear, with a horseshoe-shaped pool in the center of the plaza in front of it. In 1959, a western wing was added, which from the air made the building look like a backward 7. It was two stories tall and originally had twenty-one units, one apartment, and an office. The later addition contained seven more units, making a final total of twenty-eight. All the rooms were connected by an outdoor balcony with wrought-iron railings. The motel's roofline, the outside edge of which angled half inward and half outward, featured numerous brightly colored lights staggered along its entire length, giving the motel a carnival-like atmosphere at night. The second-floor eastern wing of the motel, located overtop of a carport on the lower level, featured a large lounge and game room, the glass walls of which angled inward toward the center and out to the roofline, creating an unusual effect similar to the angled walls of the Ebb Tide and the

The horseshoe-shaped heated pool of the Caribbean Motel at night. Kyle Weaver

Caribbean's own roofline. Completing the second level was a sundeck, overhung by an extension of the lounge's flat roof, which had large rectangular cutouts to let the sun through. This was a feature also incorporated in Bob's Big Boy Restaurants in California, designed by Wayne McAllister in the early 1950s. A seemingly unsupported circular concrete ramp connected the second-floor sundeck to the first-floor pool and patio area. It was actually supported by steel braces discreetly connected to triangular steel columns, which gave the ramp the illusion of floating in midair.

Overtop of the lounge, facing north, was the Caribbean's gigantic neon sign, designed and built by Harry Lanza of Allied Signs in Wildwood, consisting of the motel's name spelled out in large cursive letters. Before its installation, this sign started yet another debate as to just how large neon motel signs should be in the Crest. But this time, realizing the inevitable,

The Caribbean Motel's pool area from the top of its flying ramp. Kyle Weaver

The unusual see-through overhang of the Caribbean Motel's second-floor sundeck. Kyle Weaver

The interior of the second-floor lounge of the Caribbean Motel, redesigned in 2005 by interior decorator Darleen Lev.

the Crest commissioners approved an ordinance change on April 28, 1958, that permitted larger signs up to 100 square feet, such as the Caribbean's. Because of this ordinance, by the mid-1970s, the Crest—at least east of Atlantic Avenue—became a virtual neon-lit wonderland at night.

Another innovation by the Caribbean was its famous plastic palm trees. Used in 1958 to help create a tropical ambience, the trees quickly became a local joke. But within a couple decades, palm trees caught on in the local motel industry and eventually were used on almost all Wildwood motels to one extent or another, becoming a Wildwood trademark in the process.

During 1959, Lou Morey built the Chateau Bleu Motel in North Wildwood, with a unique, abstract-shaped concrete canopy overhanging the entrance to its front office, and the Chalet and Carriage Stop Motels in Wildwood Crest. The Carriage Stop, a large, T-shaped motel with a red brick veneer and gabled roof, was designed to evoke a Colonial appearance. Meanwhile, Will kept busy building the Jolly Roger Motel on Atlantic Avenue between Palm and Lotus Roads in the Crest. Another classic U-

CARIBBEAN MOTEL ROOMS

DELUXE MOTEL ROOM
SLEEPS 2-4

WINDOW

BATH

CLOSET

DOUBLE BED

TABLE

DRESSER

DOUBLE BED

TV

TABLE

WINDOW

DELUXE ONE ROOM
EFFICIENCY
SLEEPS 2-4

WINDOW

BATH

EFFICIENCY

DOUBLE BED

TABLE

CLOSET

DOUBLE BED

DRESSER

TABLE

TV

WINDOW

The two-room layouts available at the Caribbean Motel. These designs are typical of most of the mid-century motels in The Wildwoods.
Diagram by Kirk Hastings

The Caribbean Motel's huge neon sign at night.

shaped motel with a rectangular pool in the middle, the Jolly Roger
boasted a larger-than-life-size pirate figure mounted on its roof over the
office—complete with treasure chest and upraised sword.

Polynesian Pop Comes to the Jersey Shore

One of the most unusual motels constructed in 1959 was the Casa Bahama
Motel at Orchid Road and Atlantic Avenue in the Crest, built in a Polynesian style to evoke the South Seas by contractor Mike Branca, an employee
of Lou Morey, for Chester and Catherine Jastremski. This two-story, L-
shaped motel had nineteen units, a first-floor office, and living quarters
for the owners. It also featured a second-floor sundeck and a rectangular
pool in the crook of the L. Its most striking architectural feature was a series
of A-frame false fronts that made it look like a row of two-story native huts
connected together. Each wing of the L featured four of the A-frame fronts,
covered in wood shingles. A freestanding neon sign with a futuristic-
looking design recalling the modernistic automobiles of the time stood on

the northwest corner of the property. An abundance of plastic palm trees completed the ersatz Polynesian atmosphere.

The Casa Bahama was one of the first of many Polynesian Pop, or Tiki, style motels to be built in The Wildwoods. The architectural style's origins went all the way back to 1934, when Ernest Beaumont-Gantt, originally from New Orleans and popularly known as Don the Beachcomber, built the first small tiki bar on McCadden Place in Hollywood. Featuring an abundance of fake palm trees, the bar was expanded in 1937 with even more South Seas ambience, including bamboo, imported woods, tropical plants, bananas, coconuts, native weapons, flower leis, and other Polynesian paraphernalia hanging from the ceilings. It also featured original— and potent—Polynesian cocktails such as the Zombie and Tahitian Rum Punch. Beaumont-Gantt opened a second tiki bar in Chicago in 1940 and a third in Waikiki later that decade.

Victor Bergeron carried on the Tiki style with Trader Vic's in Oakland, California, in the mid-1940s. He later expanded his franchise with the Outrigger bar in Seattle in 1949. Both had a strong South Seas flavor. The

The unusual Casa Bahama Motel, at Orchid Road and Atlantic Avenue in Wildwood Crest's motel district, was built in 1959 by contractor Mike Branca (an employee of Lou Morey) who owned the motel in the late 1970s and early 1980s.

The pool and A-frame architecture of the Casa Bahama Motel.
Kyle Weaver

expanded Outrigger became Trader Vic's in 1960. During the 1950s and the 1960s, many other similar spin-off bars and lounges popped up all over the United States.

The Tiki style caught on and became somewhat of a cultural phenomenon in the country after the end of World War II, with many GIs returning home from the South Pacific area.

The Casa Bahama Motel's distinctive 1950s-style neon sign. The neon tubing has been removed from the lettering and replaced by a floodlight mounted on the pedestal. This was often done by Wildwood motel owners to save on repair costs as neon signs aged and their neon tubing fell out or no longer worked. Kyle Weaver

Decorative tiki masks hanging on an outside wall of the Casa Bahama.

Many Wildwood motels feature distinctive designs on the doors of their units, such as this one from the Casa Bahama.

James Michener's 1948 Pulitzer Prize–winning book, *Tales of the South Pacific*, helped it along considerably. The book was made into a Broadway musical in 1949 and a Cinemascope movie in 1958. It also put the term "Bali Ha'i," meaning "exotic paradise," into the common vernacular. Michener followed these books with *Return to Paradise* in 1951 and *Hawaii* in 1959.

The Tiki craze went into even higher gear when a book called *The Kon-Tiki Expedition* by Norwegian zoologist Thor Heyerdahl was published in the United States in 1950. This best-selling book was about Heyerdahl's five-month expedition with five other men across the Pacific, from the coast of Peru to the island of Tahiti, also known as French Polynesia after it became a French colony in 1880. They made the voyage in a pre-Columbian balsa log raft, named the *Kon-Tiki* after the first great chief in Tahiti. A documentary film based on the book was made in 1951 and won an Oscar for best documentary. This greatly furthered American

The Ala-Kai Motel, built in 1963 at Toledo and Atlantic Avenues in Wildwood Crest, is a great example of "Polynesian paradise" at the South Jersey shore.

interest in Polynesian lore, and many popular restaurants, bars, lounges, motels, and even bowling alleys were named Kon-Tiki in the 1950s. Heyerdahl's second book, in 1955, was *Aku Aku*, about the monolithic statues on Easter Island. This fanned even more interest in the South Seas, tiki heads, and all things Polynesian, as did the adoption of Hawaii as the fiftieth state on August 21, 1959.

The Tiki architectural style influenced the design of quite a few motels in The Wildwoods built during the 1960s, including the Ala Kai and Tahiti Motels (1963); Hawaii Kai Motel (1965); Kona Kai Motel (1968); and Royal Hawaiian and Waikiki Motels (1969), the last three designed and built by Lou Morey.

The Ash Wednesday Nor'easter of 1962

A few more motels were built during the early 1960s in The Wildwoods. But then in 1962, the three Five Mile Beach communities were suddenly forced to reevaluate all future motel construction. The reason this time was not citizen backlash. It wasn't even money. It was the weather.

On March 5, 1962, two pressure systems met off the coast of Georgia, moving slowly north and becoming a northeastern storm. When the storm reached the New Jersey coast on March 6, it stalled, held in place by a cold front moving down from Canada. Referred to later as the Ash Wednesday Nor'easter or the Great Atlantic Storm of 1962, the coastal pounding raged for three full days, producing twenty- to thirty-foot waves, eight-and-a-half-foot flood tides, and winds over fifty-eight miles per hour along the Delaware and New Jersey coasts. To make matters worse, the storm hit during the new moon, when tides were usually high to begin with.

The effects on the New Jersey barrier islands were massive beach erosion and widespread destruction of property. Many sections of the famous Wildwood Boardwalk were ripped to pieces. Most of the motels on Five Mile Beach Island that were located right on the beachfront—primarily in the Crest, such as the Beach Waves—suffered extensive damage.

After the devastation was assessed in the wake of the nor'easter, the Crest commissioners decided to install heavy bulkheads along the entire length of their beachfront to help prevent such destruction in the future from another storm. This action greatly reassured beachfront property owners, and soon construction frenzy began anew in the Crest.

The Second Motel Construction Boom

During the second half of 1962, new motels of every size, shape, and configuration began to pop up along the Wildwood Crest beachfront. Lou and Will Morey jumped right back into the swing of things that year, Lou building the Astronaut, Cara Mara, and Nomad Motels in the Crest, and Will the Flagship Motel at Lavender Road and the beach. The Buckingham Brothers, Warren and Russell, built the All Star Motel at Morning Glory Road and the beach, paying homage to various national and local sports figures.

In 1963, Lou, in partnership with fellow contractor John DeFrancesco, built his first restaurant, the nautical-looking Captain's Table, on the beachfront at Topeka Avenue in the Crest. He also somehow had the time to build the Bonanza Motel at Stockton Road and Ocean Avenue. Though named after a popular western television program airing at the time, the Bonanza, with its circular office building and huge neon sign, looked more like something from *The Jetsons*.

A block or two away, the two-story Tahiti Motel also went up in 1963, one of the best examples of Polynesian Pop architecture on the island. An L-shaped building, it featured a rectangular pool and notched rafters along the edge of its thatched roof. Both ends of the motel had large gables that suggested Polynesian huts. A freestanding neon sign topped

The Bonanza Motel, built in 1963 by Lou Morey at Stockton Road and Ocean Avenue in Wildwood Crest's motel district, was named after the western TV series that was popular at the time.

by a tiki head and surrounded by lava rocks and plastic palm trees gave it a South Pacific look.

The most significant structure built in Wildwood in 1963 was the SurfSide Restaurant, located at Lavender Road and Ocean Avenue across the street from the Caribbean Motel. Opened on July 4, 1963, by Thomas Michael John Sr., a recent immigrant from Greece known by almost everyone as Tomi John, the SurfSide was another architectural innovation. The building was roughly circular in shape, with five angled walls. A rectangular section at the back of the restaurant enclosed the kitchen area. It was topped with a multiprowed roof consisting of five triangular, peaked sections. Large plate-glass windows extended up into the angle of each prow. The underside of the roof, mostly inside the restaurant, freely displayed the steel beams and wooden rafters that supported it. The restaurant's interior was painted in bright pastel shades of yellow, orange, aqua, and tan. A U-shaped lunch counter dominated the center of the restaurant, which consisted of one large room with the kitchen area hidden behind a back wall. The counter was surrounded by individual booths arranged in geometric patterns. Large, globe-shaped light fixtures hung from the ceiling. Nautical- and tropical-themed decorations and pictures on the rear wall, which had a cutout window through which the kitchen staff could

The Tahiti Motel, built in 1963 on Atlantic Avenue in Wildwood Crest's motel district. The plastic palm trees and simulated thatched roof create a South Seas ambience on the Jersey shore. Al Alven

Tahiti Motel's attention-grabbing "tiki-style" plastic sign. Al Alven

The iconic SurfSide Restaurant, built in 1963 on Ocean Avenue at Lavender Road in Wildwood Crest, across the street from the Caribbean Motel. With its unusual multiple-prowed roof, it is a true Doo Wop classic.
Douglas Hunsberger/
Sea View Color

Early postcard art of the SurfSide Restaurant in Wildwood Crest.

pass orders, completed the Coffee Shop Modern effect. At first the population of Wildwood Crest hesitated to accept such an unusual building in their midst. But it eventually won them over and became a local landmark for many years.

The interior of the SurfSide Restaurant on a typically busy summer day. The bright colors, paneled walls, and globe lighting are all very representative of authentic early-1960s architecture. David Williams

The year 1964 saw the construction of the Admiral, Hi-Lili, Singapore, and Villa Nova Motels by Lou Morey. The main section of the Admiral Motel, which faced north, was a typical flat-roofed, four-story, rectangular building with continuous outdoor balconies and a rectangular pool in front. But its western office wing, with giant floor-to-ceiling windows, had a huge, angled, cantilevered roof in two separate sections that didn't quite meet, making the building look almost as if it were coming apart at the seams.

The Singapore, right behind the Admiral, was another groundbreaking edifice. The main section, which faced south, was a three-story, rectangular structure with continuous outdoor balconies and bright red railings. An oriental garden lay spread out in front of it, complete with exotic plants and a small Asian-style wooden bridge that arched over a creeklike extension of the cube-shaped pool. The entire courtyard was surrounded by a bright red, Far Eastern style wooden fence. The four-story western wing of the motel, which housed the office and owner's living quarters on the first

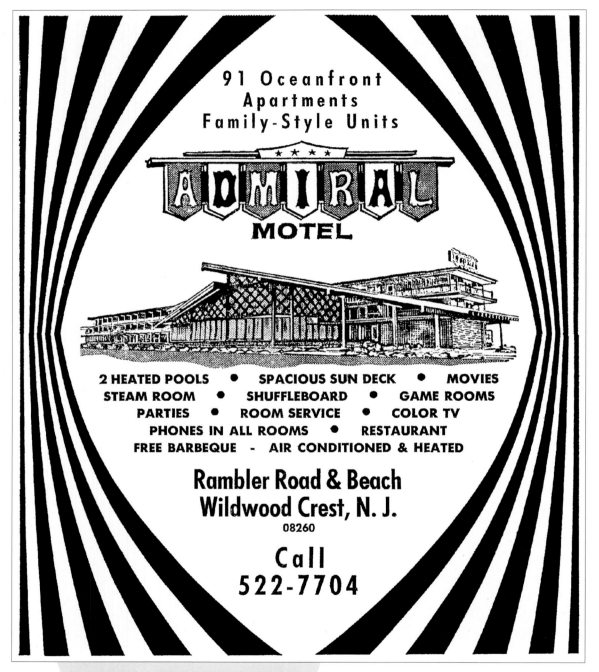

This is an original magazine ad for the Admiral Motel, published right after its construction in 1964.

The unique pagoda section of the Singapore Motel, which houses the office on the first floor and motel units on the upper floors. Kyle Weaver

The Singapore Motel, built in 1964 by Lou Morey on Orchid Road and the beach in Wildwood Crest's motel district. Kyle Weaver

The Pan American Motel was built by Will Morey in 1964 on Ocean Avenue in Wildwood Crest. The revolving plastic and metal sign on the roof was meant to bring to mind Russia's Sputnik space satellite, which ushered in the Space Age in 1957. Al Alven

floor and guest units on the upper floors, was built to resemble a giant pagoda. A large neon sign on the rooftop spelled out the name of the motel and included Asian motifs.

That same year, Will Morey built the rectangular, six-story Pan American Motel on the beachfront between Aster and Cardinal Roads in the Crest—his most ambitious construction project yet. The Pan American's design was based on that of the Americana Hotel, built in 1956 in Bal Harbour, Florida, by Morris Lapidus. It featured a large penthouse suite atop the fifth floor, where Will and his wife lived after 1964, as well as a circular pool, sundeck, restaurant, and gift shop. The open first floor served as a parking bay beneath the other floors. On top of the elevator tower was mounted a huge, sputnik-shaped globe with the red letters "Pa" on it. The interior-lit ball rotated like a real satellite, and its movement caused some consternation among local officials. Though the sign eventually was allowed to remain as it was, it became one of only two animated motel

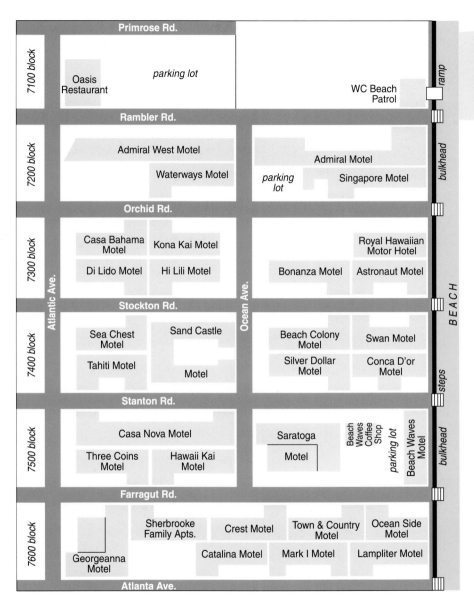

signs allowed in the Crest, the other being the revolving lighthouse atop the Cape Cod Inn a few blocks away, built in 1966.

Construction on new motels, especially in the Crest, continued throughout the next few years, although at a slightly slower pace. The year 1966 saw the construction of the Admiral Resort Motel West across the street from the original Admiral Motel, the Attaché Resort Motel, and the Yankee Clipper Motel, all designed and built by Lou Morey. In 1967, Lou built the Commander-by-the-Sea and Palm Beach Motels. During this same period, additional motels went up, such as the Fleur de Lis Motel (1966) and Granada Motel (1967), both built by John DeFrancesco, and the Frontier Motel (1966), built by Charles R. Rice.

In 1968, John DeFrancesco built the four-story, U-shaped Crusader Resort Motor Inn at Cardinal Road and Ocean Avenue on the beachfront in the Crest. Somewhat of a departure from the usual sun-sea-sand-surf motif of most Wildwood motels, the Crusader's design suggested a medieval castle. The large west wing, facing Ocean Avenue, featured a roofline embellished with a crenellated false front, and the face of the wing was covered with dark blue mosaic tiles. Different colored tiles on the wall formed the figure of a large medieval knight, one hand holding a banner

The Crusader Oceanfront Resort, built by John DeFrancesco in 1968 at Cardinal Road and Ocean Avenue in Wildwood Crest, deviates slightly from the typical Doo Wop Wildwood motel in that its theme is derived from medieval history rather than the usual sun-sea-sand-surf pattern. Al Alven

and the other resting on his sword. Next to him were two decorative medieval-style shields. A three-story-tall neon sign shaped like a castle tower spelled out "Crusader" on the Ocean Avenue side.

Lou Morey built four more motels in the Crest in 1968 and 1969, three of which reflected the still popular (at least in The Wildwoods) Tiki style of architecture. The Kona Kai Motel was the first, at Orchid Road and Ocean Avenue. Two and three stories tall, L-shaped, and featuring a rectangular pool, the east wing of the building, which housed the motel office on the first floor and units on the second, was faced with an authentic lava rock veneer, giving it a volcanic South Seas look. The entrance to the motel office was surrounded by a small tropical garden with carved wooden tiki heads of various sizes. A large neon sign on the roof spelled out the motel's name in Polynesian-style lettering. The motel looked particularly striking at night, when the tall tiki torches located around the property were lit. Its advertising material billed it as providing "A Touch of Polynesia on the Jersey Shore."

The Kona Kai Motel, built in 1968 at Orchid Road and Ocean Avenue in Wildwood Crest's motel district, features tiki torches and a tiki garden in front of the entrance to its office.

The Kona Kai Motel's Polynesian-style neon signage.

The spectacular Kona Kai Motel at night.

The next motel built by Lou was the Olympic Motor Inn at Columbine Road and Ocean Avenue. Four stories, L-shaped, and similar in appearance to the Crusader Motor Inn a couple blocks away, the Olympic, instead of a medieval knight, sported a two-dimensional, three-story-tall backlit discus thrower on the side of its western wing, painted to resemble a classic fifth century BC statue by the Greek sculptor Myron. The original figure was anatomically correct in every detail, as was the original sculpture. Mysteriously, a short time after the building's construction, the figure was suddenly sporting a strategically placed fig leaf.

The block-long Royal Hawaiian Motel on Ocean Avenue in Wildwood Crest's motel district was built in two stages by Lou Morey—the eastern wing in 1969 and the western wing in 1978. Notice the "authentic" lava rock facing on the building's walls. Kyle Weaver

In 1969, Lou designed and built the six-floor Waikiki Motor Inn at Wisteria Road and Ocean Avenue and the five-story Royal Hawaiian Motel at Orchid Road and Ocean Avenue. Both were rectangular, Polynesian-style buildings with plastic palm trees and lava rock veneers to create a South Seas atmosphere. The Waikiki featured thatched awnings and a mural of Waikiki Beach on the side of its west wing, complete with a real, three-dimensional dugout canoe. The Royal Hawaiian, named after the original on the real Waikiki Beach in Oahu, Hawaii, later doubled in size when a western extension was added by Lou in 1978.

A few more motels continued to pop up in the next few years, but by the beginning of the 1970s, the second major motel boom in The Wildwoods was just about over. According to contemporary records, by 1970 there were at least 317 motels on Five Mile Beach Island.

CHAPTER TWO

Wildwood Days (and Nights)

Because of the many big Hollywood and music industry stars that appeared regularly at Wildwood nightclubs during the 1950s and 1960s, including Don Rickles, Jerry Lewis, Tony Bennett, and the Supremes, Wildwood soon earned itself the nickname of "Little Las Vegas." But starting in the mid-1950s, Wildwood had begun to resemble Las Vegas in another way as well, with its many neon signs.

Neon was first discovered in 1898 by Sir William Ramsay and Morris W. Travers. It is an inert, odorless gas that is lighter than air, found in the earth's atmosphere and within the rocks of its crust. The French physicist Georges Claude discovered that a vapor tube filled with neon gas under low pressure produces intense orange-red light. He found that by adding small amounts of other substances to the neon tube, other colors could be produced. Argon gas, for example, creates a bluish color. Other colors could be created by painting the outside of the plastic tubing. But red has always been the most popular color for neon signs.

Immediately recognizing the value of his invention for advertising, Claude was producing successful luminous tube lighting by 1910 and had

The Bird of Paradise Motel in North Wildwood and its dazzling neon sign at night. Kyle Weaver

The Blue Marlin Motel sign in Wildwood at dusk. Kyle Weaver

the process patented in 1915. Neon signage became popular in the 1920s and was widely used in Las Vegas beginning in 1928. By the 1930s, it was everywhere, used in fluorescent lamps and electric signs. (Today it is also used as an ingredient in antifog devices and lasers.) Vapor-tube lamps make up a large class of devices that produce light by striking an arc between electrodes in a glass or plastic tube containing neon gas, gaseous sodium, or mercury.

As various nightclubs, businesses, and motels began to proliferate in The Wildwoods in the 1950s, neon became the sign of choice for them. Two neon sign companies were located in Wildwood at that time: Allied Sign Company, owned by Theodore "Ted" Polis, and Ace Sign Company, opened in 1955 by Charles Caesar, a former employee of Allied. Both had plenty of work keeping up with the demand for new signs as motels began to multiply rapidly in The Wildwoods in the 1950s. Each motel wanted its own bright, individualized sign to attract visitors. And the bigger and brighter, the better.

In March 1956, Charlie Caesar encouraged W. Robert Hentges, an employee of Allied, to come work for him at Ace. Hentges had been working for Allied since graduating from high school the previous year, and had become skilled in the profession. Not only was he an imaginative designer, but he had also learned to work capably with the plastics, sheet metal, and

The Biscayne Motel's neon sign illuminates the night on Atlantic Avenue in Wildwood Crest.

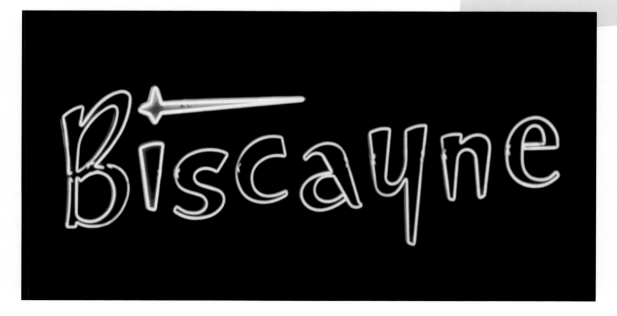

The Bel Air Motel's neon sign.

electrical components required for neon sign work. He had become proficient at building the various kinds of supports for the signs as well. Some of them had to be mounted on the roofs of buildings; some were attached to the sides; some hung from overhangs; some were freestanding. Hentges had become good at producing them all.

It wasn't long before Hentges encountered his first controversy. In 1956, Erich and Anita Jung constructed the Beach Waves Motel at Farragut Road and the beach in the Crest, the first beachfront motel on the island. For the motel, Hentges built a tall, triangular, galvanized steel tower with the words "Beach Waves Motel" in large neon letters. At the base of the tower was a series of neon waves that flashed from end to end, meeting in the middle of the sign.

Soon numerous complaints were received from nearby Crest residents about the size and brightness of the sign. In response, the borough government enacted a new ordinance regulating the size of all future neon signage and prohibiting flashing animation. That ordinance is still in effect to this day.

In the early 1960s, yet another neon sign company appeared in Wildwood: Lanza Signs, owned by Harry Lanza, who had previously worked for

The amusing sign of the Lollipop Motel,
on Atlantic Avenue in North Wildwood.
Kyle Weaver

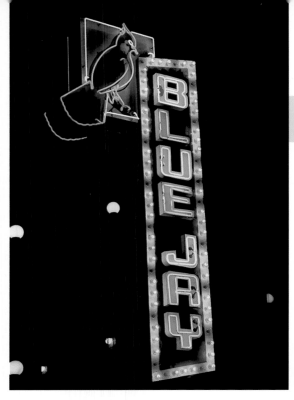

The neon sign for the Blue Jay Motel on Atlantic Avenue in Wildwood. *Kyle Weaver*

Allied. The first revolving sign in The Wildwoods was installed by Lanza Signs in 1964, on Will Morey's Pan American Motel in Wildwood Crest. The sign remains in place as of this writing. Lanza built many other classic neon signs in The Wildwoods, including the ones for the Caribbean, Armada, and Casa Bahama Motels.

Another imaginative neon sign, this one is on the roof of the Pyramid Motel, at Atlantic Avenue in Wildwood Crest.

Robert Hentges left Ace Signs in January 1964, and on February 11 of that year, he opened yet another neon sign company in The Wildwoods, called ABS Sign Company, the ABS standing for "Always Better Service." In 1965, Hentges bought Ace Sign Company and merged it with ABS. That spring, ABS installed the second revolving sign in The Wildwoods, on the Cape Cod Motel in the Crest. The sign cost $3,500 to build; today the same sign would cost in excess of $15,000. It remains in place to this day. Another ordinance enacted soon after by the Crest borough commissioners put the kibosh on any further revolving signs. So the Pan American and Cape Cod signs remain the only two.

Over the years, ABS has constructed hundreds of neon signs in The Wildwoods, including signs for the Swan, Satellite, Carousel, Crusader, and Aztec Motels. More recently, it has also built signs for the Starlux Motel and Subway restaurant, both on Rio Grande Avenue in Wildwood; the Beach Terrace Motor Inn , also in Wildwood; and the Olympic Island Beach Resort and Paradise Inn in Wildwood Crest. Many of ABS's signs were designed by Al Eichhorn, who finally retired in 1995, but it was Erik Statzell who designed the front of the Coastal Broadcasting Plaza on Pacific Avenue in Wildwood for ABS in 2003, the first time ABS was ever asked to design and execute an entire building façade.

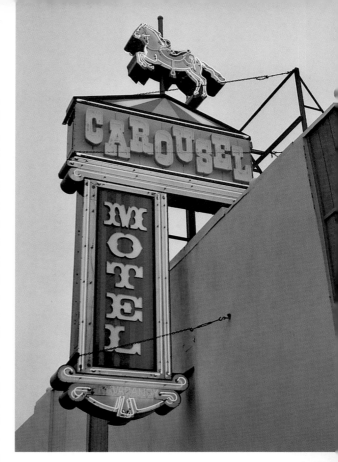

Top right: The Carousel Motel sign by ABS. Kyle Weaver

Bottom right: The American Safari Motel's original plastic sign was replaced in 2006 with a genuine neon sign built by ABS Sign Company. Kyle Weaver

In the early 1970s plastic signs came into vogue in Wildwood, as they were cheaper to build and maintain than neon. These consisted mainly of a painted plastic exterior with interior fluorescent lighting and a metal frame. But by the 1980s, neon signage had come back into vogue with a vengeance, and it has since become a large part of the modern Doo Wop revolution in Wildwood.

Today Randy Hentges, Robert's son, owns and operates ABS, which designs and builds most of the newer neon signs in town and continues to refurbish many of the older signs built by other companies, such as those on the Caribbean and Bel Air Motels. In 2006, it did a complete restoration of the neon sign for the Armada Motel in the Crest and created a new neon sign for the American Safari Motel, which previously had a painted plastic one.

CHAPTER THREE

A Summer Place

On Friday, June 6, 1958, the Caribbean Motel opened in Wildwood Crest. Its owners, Dominic and Julie Rossi, wanted to give it a South Pacific ambience, so they came up with what was then a novel idea: put palm trees around the property.

Now that wasn't as easy as it sounds. Palm trees require a tropical climate, but Wildwood's summers are only three months long, and the island can experience temperatures as low as the teens during its long winters. How could a palm tree survive in such a climate?

Simply put, it couldn't. So the Rossis came up with an innovative answer: They made their own palm trees out of plastic.

This solution helped give guests at the Caribbean the feeling that they really were vacationing at a South Seas paradise, but the Rossis also took their share of ribbing from local residents for the artificial foliage. A few years later, however, Ron Berg, a local police officer and owner of the Mariner Motel in the Crest, decided he liked the artificial palms and started experimenting with making some for his own motel. They turned out so well that soon other motel owners with tropical themes began to ask Ron for copies.

The "official tree" of The Wildwoods, *Palmus plasticus wildwoodii.*

The Caribbean Motel was the first motel in The Wildwoods to use plastic palm trees.

Decades later, in 1984, Bob Belansen of the Bristol Plaza Motor Inn in the Crest attended the annual Philadelphia Home Show, where he spotted a display with artificial palm trees that were better made and more realistic than any he had seen before. He learned that the trees had been made by A. Edward Hiller of Langhorne, Pennsylvania. In the summer of 1980, Ed, who had spent some time in Orlando, Florida, while in the army, decided he wanted an artificial palm tree to decorate his backyard pool area. At that time, there were none available commercially, so Ed set about building his own. After some experimentation, he found that he could construct very realistic and durable artificial palms with trunks of fiberglass and fronds of a custom-made polyethylene plastic with a UV stabilizer to protect them from harsh weather conditions such as bright sunshine, wind, and salt air. By 1982, Ed, who had previously run an office-cleaning business, was making the artificial palms full-time, supplying them to individuals, restaurants, malls, swim clubs, water-slide parks, and amusement parks. Initially his four sons, Pat, Mike, Joe, and Bubs, assisted him with the manufacture and sale of the trees, so he called his business 4 Sons Custom Palm Trees.

Bob Belansen immediately ordered some of the trees for his Crest motel, and pretty soon many other Wildwood motels were ordering them as well. Thus a cottage industry was born. But for a short time in the late 1980s, strange-looking palm trees with fuzzy leaves began to appear in Wildwood and still can be seen in motel brochures of the period. These were actually Ed's trees too, and he explains their strange appearance: "Though the palm trunks come with a lifetime guarantee, after a summer or two of use the palm fronds would wear out. Some Wildwood motel owners at the time being a little tight with a penny, instead of ordering replacement leaves from me, many of them just stuck the branches from their artificial Christmas trees into the palm trunks. It made for a pretty unusual-looking tree!"

With the Doo Wop revolution in Wildwood in 1998, Ed's business boomed. On Saturday, July 15, 2000, New Jersey governor Christine Todd Whitman "planted" one of Ed's artificial palms next to the pool area of the new Starlux Motel at the motel's dedication and declared the plastic palm the "official tree" of The Wildwoods. In her honor, the Starlux tree was named the *Palmus*

Ed Hiller of 4 Sons Custom Palm Trees, "planting" another tropical beauty at the Diamond Crest Motel in Wildwood Crest.

Decorative cornerpiece of the Rio Motel, right across the street from the Newport Motel on Rio Grande Avenue in Wildwood.

plasticarum whitmana, but later the genus became known by its more generic name of *Palmus plasticus wildwoodii.*

Ed says that Wildwood makes up only about 10 percent of his total business today, though this still amounts to hundreds of new palm trees a year, and he sells his trees in more than forty-five states, as well as the Far East, Canada, and several European countries. Only one son, Patrick, still helps with the business; the others have since moved on to other enterprises, but he still gets help occasionally from George "Dirty Harry" Marino, a long-time employee. He has four tree sizes, ranging from seven to twenty-four feet tall, the most popular of which is nine feet. His typical tree has fourteen to fifteen fronds, which come in four different styles. Prices range from about $400 to $1,200. Fake coconuts are available for an extra charge.

Though Ed's 3,200-square-foot shop is situated next to a cornfield in Bucks County, Pennsylvania, he makes frequent trips to The Wildwoods each spring to install new trees and refurbish old ones. He used to charge $10 each to remove palm leaves in the fall so that they could be stored during Wildwood's harsh winters and reinstall them in the spring, but he no longer offers this service—a concession to his advancing age. Motel owners must now remove and replace their own fronds each year. When asked whether he plans to retire anytime soon, Ed, who is now in his early seventies, replies that he intends to keep making and selling his palm trees as long as he is physically able. "I got my job, my business, and my hobby all rolled into one," he says. "I just love it."

CHAPTER FOUR

I Get Around

The Society for Commercial Archeology (SCA) was founded in Vermont in 1977 by a small group of scholars who were interested in studying and preserving roadside architecture, historic twentieth-century structures such as old diners, motels, gas stations, and their related signage. After incorporating in 1979, they formed a board of directors and set about actively pursuing their interests in locations around the country.

The members of the SCA discovered Wildwood and its trove of mid-century motels and structures, still standing much as they had been since the late 1950s and early 1960s, on a board retreat in June 1983, after being invited to the island by Wildwood's director of public relations, Vic DiSylvester. They were astounded to find that such a concentration of mid-century motel architecture, neon signs and all, still existed in the country. Most had already fallen to the wrecking ball.

The result of that retreat was a small publication called *Wildwood Workbook*, describing the unique buildings and geographic features of the island in loving detail. One of the writers of that booklet was Steven Izenour, an architect and Yale University graduate who had been associated with the renowned Venturi, Scott Brown architectural firm in Philadelphia since

1969. Besides being an architectural school professor at the University of Pennsylvania, Izenour had previously studied the architecture of Las Vegas and Atlantic City and written books on both.

Izenour didn't know it at the time, but his association with Wildwood and its mid-century motels was just beginning.

Doo Wop Trolley Tours

Chuck Schumann grew up in Wildwood Crest in the 1950s and 1960s, and except for some time in Florida going to marine biology school, he has spent his entire life in Wildwood. As a teenager, he worked for Otto Stocker, who owned and ran the *Sightseer* cruise boat out of Otten's Harbor. When Otto retired, Chuck took over the ownership of the *Sightseer*. Now, every summer, he captains three sightseeing cruises a day in and around Wildwood's waters and back bays.

Early in 1991, Chuck went to the powers-that-be at the Mid-Atlantic Center for the Arts (MAC) in Cape May. MAC had been the primary force

The Imperial 500 Motel, built in 1964 on Atlantic Avenue in Wildwood Crest. Kyle Weaver

The American Safari Motel, at Lavender Road and Ocean Avenue in Wildwood Crest, was built in the early 1960s. It was originally called the Safari Motel. Kyle Weaver

in the early 1970s that had helped restore and revitalize Cape May's Victorian architecture, eventually making the city a national historic site. Chuck suggested that MAC sponsor some kind of architectural and historical trolley tour of The Wildwoods and showed the board members various photos of Wildwood buildings. Most of the photos were of late-Victorian and early-twentieth-century structures, but with a few 1950s and 1960s buildings mixed in.

Two of the board members, executive director Michael Zuckerman and vice president Elan Zingman-Leith, who had also been involved with the restoration efforts of the 1930s Art Deco building district in South Beach, Florida, in the late 1970s, were intrigued. After doing their own "windshield survey" of The Wildwoods, they became convinced that the 1950s and 1960s structures were far more significant than the earlier ones, and that there were indeed enough of them to warrant a themed trolley tour.

During the spring of 1991, the two men and Elan's wife, Suzie, came up with a tour script, with significant local history input from Chuck Schumann. Not liking the standard architectural terms Populuxe or Googie, which were popularly used at the time for such structures, the group came up with the distinctive term "Doo Wop," taken from the musical style that had dominated the Philadelphia and South Jersey cultural scene in the late 1950s and early 1960s. They also decided to create labels for the different styles of Doo Wop architecture:

- **Modern**: A style featuring large glass walls that evoke the jet-age airports of the 1950s and 1960s. Examples: the Fantasy and Admiral Motels.
- **Vroom!**: A style where movement is expressed in the architecture through forward-thrusting, pointed building parts. Examples: the Ebb Tide and Rio Motels.
- **Polynesian Pop or Tiki**: A style featuring thatched roofs, plastic palm trees, beanpole tiki torches, and Kon-Tiki heads, recalling the film *South Pacific.* Examples: the Waikiki, Tahiti, Kona Kai, and Casa Bahama Motels.
- **Phony Colonee**: A style featuring the look of early Colonial buildings, with lots of brick and Early American style lampposts. Examples: the Saratoga and Carriage Stop Motels.
- **Chinatown Revival**: A style that brings exotic, faraway, Asian destinations to the Jersey Shore. Example: the Singapore Motel.

Doo Wop Architecture Styles

◀ Modern
The Admiral Motel (later the Oceanview Motel) was built in 1964 by Lou Morey at Rambler and Ocean Avenues in Wildwood Crest. It is dominated by a unique angled roof design, characteristic of the Modern style.
Al Alven

◀ Vroom!
The oldest section of the Rio Motel, built in 1958 by Ben Schlenzig on Rio Grande Avenue in Wildwood, exhibits the thrusting points of the Vroom! style.

▼ Polynesian Pop or Tiki
Though its name refers to islands in the Caribbean, the Casa Bahama Motel is an outstanding example of the Polynesian Pop or Tiki style of Doo Wop architecture with odd A-frame roofs thrown in for good measure.

▲ Phony Colonee
The Carriage Stop Motel, built in 1959 by Morey Brothers Builders at St. Paul and Atlantic Avenues in Wildwood Crest, is a perfect example of what later came to be called the Phony Colonee style of Doo Wop architecture.

◀ Chinatown Revival
The Singapore Motel exemplifies the Chinatown Revival style of Doo Wop architecture. In its early days it even featured its own oriental garden.

Launched with much fanfare, the Doo Wop '50s Trolley Tour began on June 28, 1991. Chuck Schumann had made arrangements with Jack Morey of the Morey Organization, which owned, among other things, the Seapointe Village development at the southern end of Wildwood Crest, to use Seapointe's shuttle trolley. The tour had a very successful first season—so successful that Barbara Waterman, owner-operator of the Atlantic Motel and Restaurant in Wildwood, succeeded in persuading the Wildwood city council to institute a 1950s Weekend in September of that year, the first of what was planned to be an annual event.

The tour continued through the summer of 1992. That same summer a Historic American Buildings Survey (HABS) was commissioned of the Caribbean Motel in Wildwood Crest, sponsored by the National Park Service and the Department of the Interior, perhaps inspired by the *Wildwood Workbook* produced by the Society for Commercial Archeology back in 1983. A detailed survey and history of the Caribbean was written by Alison Isenberg, a student at the University of Pennsylvania, and the study was permanently archived in the HABS survey file in the Library of Congress in Washington, D.C. It was not the last time Wildwood's motels would be studied by university students.

Midway through the summer season of 1993, the Doo Wop Trolley Tour was suddenly suspended. Ridership had dropped, and the Seapointe's trolley was now no longer available. But the tour had put Wildwood's Doo Wop architecture on the map, and subsequent developments throughout the next few years would bring it back into focus in a big way.

The Moreys Get Involved in Doo Wop

During the mid-1990s, a group of Disney World executives spent a significant amount of time in Wildwood, doing research for a proposed Boardwalk Hotel at their resort. On one last trip to The Wildwoods before the opening of their hotel, Charlie Hardiman, the general manager of the project, brought almost his entire executive board along with him. Dane Wells, an ardent preservationist, ex-president of the Cape May County Chamber of Commerce, and owner of the Queen Victoria Inn bed-and-breakfast in Cape May, was asked to provide them with some suitable entertainment. Though by this time the Doo Wop '50s Trolley Tour had been suspended, Wells talked Michael Zuckerman into dusting it off once again and taking Hardiman and his crew along. The board members all loved it.

Word of this tour later got back to Jack Morey and his brother, Will Morey Jr., who were the heads of the Morey Organization in Wildwood. Will Morey Sr., Jack and Will's father, and his brother Bill had formed the organization back in 1969 after buying the old Surfside Pier at 26th Street and the Boardwalk in North Wildwood and renaming it Morey's Pier. The success of this venture led them to buy the old Marine Pier at Schellenger Avenue and the Boardwalk in Wildwood in 1978. This was rechristened Mariner's Landing Pier. A decade and two water parks later, the Morey Organization had become a major financial and cultural force in The Wildwoods.

Jack and Will called Dane Wells and asked him what interest Disney had in The Wildwoods. Wells told them about the Boardwalk Hotel and said

Mariner's Landing, today part of Morey's Piers.
Kyle Weaver

that the Disney executives simply liked Wildwood's 1950s and 1960s architecture. So the tour had seemed like a good idea.

A few days later, Jack and Will met with Wells in the dining room of the Queen Victoria Inn. Wells told them he felt that The Wildwoods had a great theme going for them, focusing on the fifties and sixties. But the Morey brothers were skeptical. How could that possibly compete with the quaint, romantic Victorian theme of Cape May?

Wells pointed to a huge portrait of Queen Victoria hanging on the wall. "Look at her, all dressed in mourning black, and among her favorite phrases was 'We are not amused,'" Wells replied. He went on to say that Cape May had been pretty clever in turning the era bearing her name into such a fun and romantic theme. He then rattled off the things that are associated with the 1950s, such as the birth of television; the genesis of rock and roll; GIs returning from the war and building homes for their new families; and the beginning of the Space Age.

"What a theme!" Wells concluded. "It makes Victoriana look dour."

Wells then referred the Morey brothers to Steve Izenour, an old acquaintance of his through the Society for Commercial Archeology. The Moreys lost no time in contacting Izenour at the University of Pennsylvania. They found out that Izenour had already been in Wildwood in 1983 with the SCA, and that a publication called *Wildwood Workbook* had resulted. The booklet spoke of the importance of preserving Wildwood's fifties and sixties architecture and was apparently the first publication of its kind. Izenour was only too glad, at the Moreys' insistence, to take another look at Wildwood's unique buildings.

That meeting changed Jack Morey's mind about Wildwood's midcentury buildings. From that point forward, he became a true believer in the Doo Wop cause. And so did Izenour.

CHAPTER FIVE

Rescue Me

After their initial meeting, Jack Morey retained Steve Izenour's services so that Steve could come up with a plan to combine two of the Morey Organization's 1960s properties—the Port Royal and Jolly Roger Motels in Wildwood Crest—into one huge, reinvented Doo Wop megaresort. This planned renovation never came about, but it gave Izenour an idea. Why not encourage some of his university's architectural students to come to Wildwood and study the town's unique buildings?

By early 1997, Izenour had persuaded University of Pennsylvania and Kent State University to send some of their architectural students to Wildwood to study the Doo Wop buildings and present suggestions as to how they might be protected and preserved in the future. Jack Morey was thrilled with the idea—so thrilled that he kicked in $15,000 in order to help fund the study.

So in February 1997, a number of students from Kent State arrived in Wildwood to begin their work. Izenour directed the effort, assisted by Daniel Vieyra, one of Kent State's architecture professors. Their overall purpose was to document Wildwood's mid-century buildings for the Library of Congress. Izenour had done pretty much the same thing in Las Vegas in

1968, documenting that town's unique buildings and publishing a booklet recording the results called *Learning from Las Vegas*.

The students were fascinated with Wildwood. So was Vieyra. The incredible proliferation of neon signage, boomerang rooflines, Tomorrowland ramps, *Jetson* fins, floating balconies, tiki heads, and leaning walls all in one place completely amazed them. It was like stepping back in time to the 1950s and 1960s. Wildwood was a living time capsule of postwar architecture.

More than perhaps any other building, the Caribbean Motel in Wildwood Crest was considered by the students to be an almost perfect example of Doo Wop architecture, with its huge neon sign, horseshoe-shaped pool, leaning windows on its second-floor lounge, and curving concrete ramp that connected the lounge to the pool area. The students were so enamored of it that three from Kent State decided to draw up detailed blueprints of the Caribbean property in the spring of 1997 as part of the Historic American Buildings Survey, number NJ-1186.

The Caribbean—a subject for study by scholars of architecture. Kyle Weaver

In September of that year, a number of architecture students from the University of Pennsylvania Graduate School of Fine Arts arrived in Wildwood to join in the Kent State study. This group was headed by architectural historian George Thomas. In short order, they became as enthralled by Wildwood as the Kent State students had.

With all the attention being lavished on the town by dozens of Ivy League university students, Dan Vieyra persuaded the Society for Commercial Archeology to return to Wildwood once again and hold its 20th Anniversary Conference there. During the weekend of September 18–21, a number of people who were prominent in national architectural circles came to Wildwood and spoke at the conference, including Alan Hess, who had written the book *Googie* in 1985, and Thomas Hine, who wrote *Populuxe* in 1986. Izenour and Vieyra also delivered speeches.

On January 16, 1998, the Penn and Kent State University students, who were now collectively referred to as the Wildwood Studio, presented some of the results of their studies to the public for the first time at the Doo Wop Preservation League's headquarters at Pine and Pacific Avenues in Wildwood. In what was billed as a "midterm working session," the students displayed their work and invited input from locals. The event proved to be popular with Wildwood residents and was well attended.

The following spring, Izenour succeeded in bringing yet another contingent of university students to Wildwood to study its buildings, this time from Yale, Izenour's alma mater. The Wildwood Convention and Business Bureau kicked in another $15,000 to fund this group's studies, and suddenly The Wildwoods were the architectural focus of the nation. Articles on Wildwood's buildings began to appear regularly in national magazines and newspapers. "Must-see Americana . . . a paradise of plastic palms and flamboyant motels," declared *U.S. News and World Report.* "A drive down Ocean Avenue is a drive through beach blanket bingo territory, a stretch of screamingly retro motels," said *USA Today.* "A unique architectural trove of seaside boardwalk-town architecture from 1950 to 1965, the last golden age of America's endless summers," touted the *New York Times.* Many other articles appeared in publications such as the *Baltimore Sun,* the *Los Angeles Times,* the *Washington Post, Newsweek,* and *Smithsonian* magazine.

During the summer of 1998, even the Doo Wop '50s Trolley Tour was revived by MAC and began to operate again for the first time since 1993. It still runs every summer as of this writing.

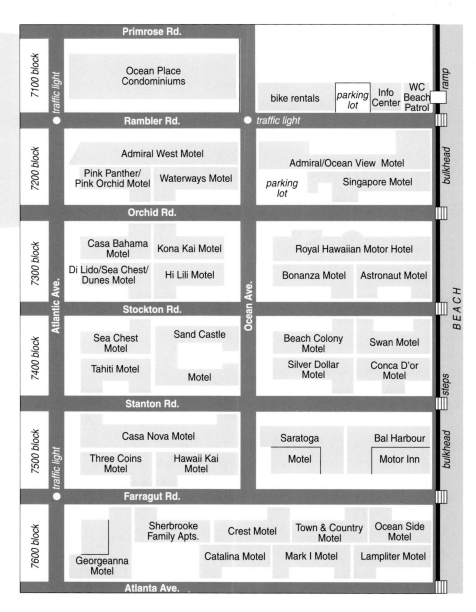

A diagram of Wildwood Crest's beachfront Motel District as it looked, virtually unchanged, from 1978 to 2001. Featuring ten solid blocks of individually owned mid-century-style Doo Wop motels, for more than twenty years this unique district was the only one of its kind in the world.

Diagram by Kirk Hastings

On the weekend of May 12–13, 1998, the completed booklet *Learning from the Wildwoods: A Research Studio,* directly inspired by Izenour's *Learning from Las Vegas,* was finally unveiled to the public at the Doo Wop League's headquarters. Faculty advisors listed for the project were Steven

Izenour, Michael Haverland, Maria Lindenfeldar, Timothy Kearney, and Daniel Vieyra. In the booklet, the students of Kent, Penn, and Yale examined all aspects of The Wildwoods related to popular culture, such as its expansive beach, its funky Boardwalk, its neon signage, its main streets, the gateways to the island, and of course, its motels. Two of its foremost recommendations: "Make no small signs" and "You can't plant too many plastic palms!"

Architectural historian George Thomas contributed to the booklet as well, with his dissertation called "The Wildwoods-by-the-Sea: Learning from 'Other-Directed Style,'" referring to a previous essay published in 1958 by cultural geographer J. B. Jackson. In that piece, Jackson had stated that the "new, modern vacation style" was all about flashiness: "a flashiness of color and design . . . neon lights, floodlights, fluorescent lights, spotlights, moving and changing lights of every strength and color—they constitute one of the most original and potentially creative elements in the 'other directed' style. It would be hard to find a formula for obliterating the workaday world and substituting that of the holiday than this: Nighttime and a garden of moving, colored lights . . . The neon light is one of the great artistic innovations of our age." Jackson might well have been describing The Wildwoods, for his description was amazingly similar to what actually existed there at the time.

The Wildwood Studio and its students had made a significant impact on the residents of The Wildwoods, and their presence had brought national attention to Wildwood's aging mid-century architecture. But would their involvement be enough to save those forty-year-old buildings from the inevitable encroachment of progress?

Doo Wop Preservation and the Starlux

During the winter of 1995–96, Jack Morey got together with Chuck Schumann and suggested that they try to form some kind of organization that might be able to help promote and preserve the mid-century motels and buildings in Wildwood, based on Steve Izenour's warning that if Wildwood natives weren't careful, they could end up "robbing future generations of a page of architectural history."

The original group started out as an unofficial, loose confederation of a few people that were interested in the future of The Wildwoods. It took two more years before they were able to incorporate and achieve official not-for-profit status. The initial board members after the 1997 incorporation consisted of Jack Morey, who became the president; B. Michael Zuckerman of MAC; Chuck Schumann; Clark Doran, an employee of the Morey Organization; Jay Ford, president of Crest Savings Bank; Ron Nardi; Steve Izenour; Elan Zingman-Leith; and Dan Vieyra. Local attorney Frank Corrado helped Zuckerman come up with the new organization's bylaws. The group promptly rented space in an empty building on the corner of Pine and Pacific Avenues in Wildwood to use as official headquarters.

A number of meetings and events were held at this location over the next couple years, including the "Learning from The Wildwoods" seminars in 1998. The group even began to collect artifacts related to Wildwood's Doo Wop history, such as 1950s Danish Modern furniture, lamps, and old neon signs from local motels. This material eventually led to a Doo Wop Museum that opened to the public in November 2000.

During July 2000, eight more Kent State students, at the behest of Steve Izenour, returned to The Wildwoods. In cooperation with the members of the Doo Wop Preservation League, they came up with "The 10 Commandments for Creating a Great Doo Wop Inspired Motel" to encourage local motel owners to refurbish and expand their properties instead of selling them or tearing them down:

Take a simple two- to three-story bar or L-shaped motel building and add the following:

1. A great name that evokes the '50s—The Rock-N-Roll Motel; a distant exotic vacation spot—The Caribbean Motel; or the space age—The Astro Motel.
2. Create a wild and crazy high reader sign with shapes and typefaces that evoke the name, e.g., stars, planets, kidney shapes, and lots and lots of neon.
3. Create a motel office, lounge, etc. in the shape of some wonderful wacky image, e.g., a spaceship, a beach ball, a sailboat, etc. with lots of color, glass and a decorative paint job.
4. Create a pool area with kidney-shaped pool surrounded by bright green Astroturf, and wild and crazy beach umbrellas and landscape with plastic palm trees.
5. Create a colorful and distinctive profile for the balcony railings—S-curves, C-curves, the more curvy the better.
6. Create an exterior color scheme made up of '50s colors, e.g., pinks, baby blue, turquoise, sea greens, for rails, doors, trim and the drapes in the picture windows.

7. Create an interior color scheme using a similar but more subtle palette, and add Jetson decorations and furnishings from the '50s.
8. Create a wild and crazy neon roof sign in the style and typeface of the motel name and high reader sign.
9. Create a decorative night lighting scheme, e.g., linear neon fascia or eave lights, floodlighting, and thematic, decorative fixtures in the pool and parking areas.
10. And last, but not least, pull this all together in an idiosyncratic, original and crazy way that clashes, jumps and jives!

The Starlux Motel, built in 2000 at Atlantic and Rio Grande Avenues in Wildwood from the remnants of the old Wingate Motel, was designed by Philadelphia architect Richard Stokes and was the first example of Neo-Doo Wop architecture in The Wildwoods. Al Alven

The year before, Jack Morey had already decided to put his money where his mouth was. Enlisting an old friend of his family as a partner, he bought the old Wingate Motel at Atlantic and Rio Grande Avenues in Wildwood. Located along the main entranceway to The Wildwoods, the Wingate had seen better days since being built in 1953 by Lewes D. Wingate. With only twenty-four units and no pool, it was never considered one of the more luxurious motels in town. Morey decided to enlist the services of architect Richard Stokes to design an extensive makeover for the property. Stokes, who was now the head of his own architectural firm in Philadelphia, had been one of the Kent State students in Wildwood back in 1997.

Stokes took "The 10 Commandments for Creating a Great Doo Wop Inspired Motel" to heart. First he added another floor and expanded the motel to thirty-six units. Then he tore down the separate office building, an

The lobby building of the Starlux Motel, showing its retro 1950s-style angled roof.
Al Alven

old Victorian-style house, and replaced it with a new Doo Wop style lounge, featuring large plate-glass windows and a swooping, geometric-shaped roof. He moved the parking lot across Atlantic Avenue and replaced the original lot with a large, kidney-shaped pool. He also added plenty of shiny aluminum, neon signage, and plastic palm trees. New Jersey governor Christine Todd Whitman visited Wildwood to dedicate the new Starlux Motel on its opening day, July 15, 2000.

The new century began a pivotal period in the history of The Wildwoods. During the summer of 2001, the Doo Wop Preservation League enlisted the services of Nancy Zerbe, the president of ARCH[2], an organization out of Metuchen, New Jersey, that provided cultural resources consultants for archeology and architectural history. Zerbe's job was to put together an application for the National Register of Historic Places for Wildwood Crest's mid-century Doo Wop motel district, which stretched along Ocean and Atlantic Avenues practically from one end of the Crest to the other. This would involve coming up with detailed descriptions of all the motels in that district, which at that time totaled more than eighty structures. Stephanie M. Hoagland, a graduate student at Columbia University, assisted with the survey fieldwork.

"This is not some big art project," Jack Morey assured Wildwood's natives. "This is a community-planning project about higher profitability and a better sense of community. The only way Doo Wop will be successful is if motel owners can make money with it."

The Starlux Motel's distinctive pool, with boomerang shapes painted on the bottom.

Paradise Lost

A series of setbacks concerning the preservation of Wildwood's motels began when Steve Izenour, in his early sixties, suddenly passed away on August 22.

Then the real estate developers started coming to the island. At first they were welcomed, as initially they targeted many of the old, rundown rooming houses in the city of Wildwood that had definitely seen better days, tearing them down and replacing them with clean, modern condo buildings. It gave the island a much-needed facelift—not to mention a financial shot in the arm. The Wildwoods, especially Wildwood City, had fallen on hard times during the eighties and nineties. Though its clean, wide beach and bustling Boardwalk still attracted thousands of visitors every summer, Wildwood's infrastructure had deteriorated significantly since the salad days of the fifties and sixties. Its once-thriving downtown area had become almost a ghost town, with many of its old shops and businesses closed and boarded up.

Next the developers started eyeing the motel properties on the island. Many of those buildings were more than forty years old, badly in need of repair and situated on land that was now much more valuable than the structures sitting on them. A good number of the motel operators were the original owners, now in their sixties and seventies. A lucrative buyout that could finance their well-deserved retirement years was a powerful incentive to forgo repairing their buildings and sell out. And many of them did.

In September 2002, it was announced that the SurfSide Restaurant in the Crest had been sold, and that in the fall it would be torn down to make room for an addition to the Water's Edge Motel next door. Tomi John Sr., who had owned and operated the restaurant since 1963, had recently died and his son Michael had decided to sell the building.

Panic spread throughout the ranks of the Doo Wop Preservation League—and the local media as well. "The enemy of neat, old architecture at the New Jersey shore is popularity and a good real-estate market. The

Wildwoods are again proving that axiom," said the editorial page of the *Atlantic City Press* on September 22. "When that happens, look out: Charming older buildings fall. Cookie-cutter condos and high rises proliferate."

In response, Jack Morey came up with a daring plan. He found out that for $20,000, it would be possible for builders to carefully dismantle the building so that it could be reassembled somewhere else later. Less than a month before the SurfSide's scheduled October 15 demolition, Morey appealed to the public for the money to help save the classic building for future reconstruction, possibly as a Doo Wop Museum, elsewhere on the island.

The situation appeared hopeless. Right up to the last day before demolition was to take place, less than half the money needed to save the building had been raised. It looked as if the SurfSide would be lost forever.

But then on October 14, the rest of the money came in. The property's new owners agreed to allow the building to be dismantled instead of demolished. Further, the Crest commissioners agreed to eventually have

The brightly-painted SurfSide Restaurant in Wildwood Crest was dismantled and saved for future reassembly.

the building reassembled farther south at Rambler Road and the beach, in the heart of the Crest's Doo Wop motel district, as a combination information center and museum.

The Preservation League members' relief over their victory was sadly short-lived. Even as the league was still trying to gain historic status for many of Wildwood's motels, they began to be torn down all over the island. During 2003, a number of them fell to the wrecking ball. One day they were there, the next they were gone. It happened that quickly.

"An awful lot of demolitions have taken place recently," bemoaned Jack Morey in an article on Wildwood's Doo Wop motels in the June 2003 issue of *Smithsonian* magazine. "If the big guys eat the little guys, then the Wildwoods lose their character and might as well be anyplace." Joe Salerno, owner of the Imperial 500 Motel in the Crest, complained, "I'm not against progress. I'm against poor planning."

The Chateau Bleu, built in 1959 by Lou Morey at 9th and Surf Avenues in North Wildwood, was placed on the New Jersey State Register of Historic Places in 2003. Al Alven

The Ebb Tide Motel, a victim of the developers.

On September 17, 2003, there was one bright spot: The Chateau Bleu Motel at 9th and Surf Avenues in North Wildwood, built in 1959 by Lou Morey, was placed on the New Jersey State Register of Historic Places. It was the first building in The Wildwoods to achieve historic status.

Just three months later, however, The Wildwoods lost one of its most widely recognized examples of classic Doo Wop architecture: the Ebb Tide Motel at Heather Road and Atlantic Avenue in the Crest. In a letter to *The Wildwood Leader* newspaper, architect Michael Hirsch lamented, "In the United States you can travel to Miami, Charleston, or Williamsburg to see architecture of other eras that has been preserved with respect for history. Future generations will only have photos of what Wildwood Crest was like: its oldest [Doo Wop] motel is gone forever."

The demolitions continued throughout 2004 at an even more rapid pace. The Casa Nova, Three Coins, Town & Country, and Crest Motels all went down early in the year in Wildwood Crest. In June, Jay's Motel in Wildwood, the first motel built on the island, was demolished. In October, the Satellite Motel in the Crest was razed. The Satellite had been featured in a number of national newspaper and magazine articles in recent years as the quintessential Wildwood Doo Wop motel. It was even featured prominently in Thomas Hine's book *Populuxe* in 1986. But by the end of October 2004, all that remained was an empty lot. It was soon followed in December by the Carousel Motel, which in its 1960s heyday had been host to

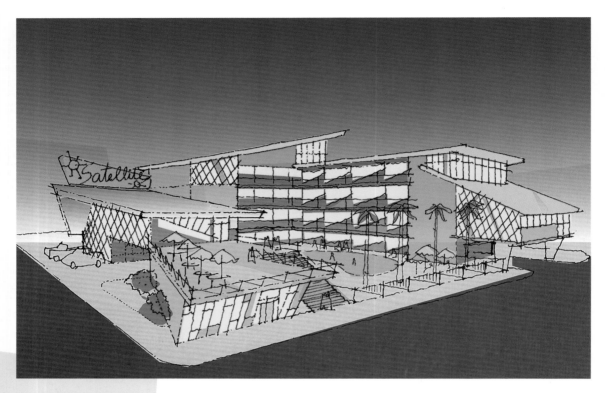

A 2004 drawing rendered by Philadelphia architect Tony Bracali, theorizing what an expansion and upgrading of the Satellite Motel might have looked like. Unfortunately, it never came to be. Anthony Bracali Architecture

celebrities such as Liberace, Connie Francis, and Johnny Mathis, and the Tahiti Motel, a classic Polynesian-style building, both in the Crest.

"This disturbs me a great deal," declared Wildwood Crest mayor John Pantalone. "None of us are enthused about these places coming down. It's just getting too much."

But the year 2005 saw the same sad pattern continue unabated. In February, the Casa Bahama Motel in the Crest was leveled. In April, exactly forty-nine years after its grand opening, the Fantasy Motel in Wildwood—the building that had marked the beginning of the Doo Wop era in The Wildwoods back in 1956—came tumbling down. This was followed by the demise of the Breezy Corner and Monta Cello Motels in the Crest that summer. In August, the half-block-long Rio Motel on the beachfront at Rio Grande Avenue in Wildwood was demolished. Originally built by Ben Schlenzig, it had been a local landmark on the main boulevard into town since 1958. Now, for the first time since its construction in 2000, the Starlux Motel, which had stood right behind the Rio, could boast of an unobstructed ocean view.

A postcard circulated during the summer of 2004 in an attempt to save the Satellite Motel from impending demolition. Regrettably, the effort was not successful.
Michael L. Hirsch Collection

The final demolition of the Satellite Motel in October 2004.

In January 2006, the Art Deco style Shore Theater in downtown Wild-wood, built way back in 1939, saw its final days before being reduced to a huge pile of rubble. That same month saw the destruction of the old Hialeah Motel, known for one summer as the new Carousel Motel after the demise of its former namesake, and the Kona Kai Motel, both in Wild-wood Crest.

The year 2006 marked exactly fifty years since the Doo Wop motel era had first begun in The Wildwoods. It also marked the final demise of the application for historic status for the Crest's Doo Wop motel district. By 2006, after four years of demolitions, there were not enough classic mid-century motels left to qualify it as a cohesive historic district.

CHAPTER SIX

The Beat Goes On

At the same time that The Wildwoods were losing their original Doo Wop structures of the fifties and sixties, an interesting countermovement started to gain momentum.

It began in 2000 with the construction of the Starlux Motel. The Doo Wop Preservation League immediately dubbed the new motel Neo–Doo Wop, the term referring to new buildings constructed with retro 1950s or 1960s Doo Wop elements incorporated into their design. One of Jack Morey's stated purposes for building the Starlux was to encourage the owners of other older Wildwood motels to also enlarge and renovate their properties, and in the process make them even *more* retro than before, instead of selling them or having them torn down. Though for the most part this hoped-for result did not materialize because of the costs involved, the construction of the Starlux did manage to start a new trend in The Wildwoods: newer buildings being constructed in the older retro style of the original Doo Wop properties.

The Doo Wop Preservation League loved the idea. If The Wildwoods couldn't maintain their individuality as a retro-style mid-century resort by

Wildwood's Boardwalk is lined with old and new Doo Wop neon signs. Kyle Weaver

saving and updating their older buildings, they could construct new ones in the same older style.

The idea struck a chord locally, and it quickly caught on. At about the same time that the Starlux opened, a new restaurant and nightclub opened in downtown Wildwood called Maureen's Restaurant and Martini Bar. The establishment's interior sported a retro 1960s look, and a large neon palm tree adorned the front façade. Michael Hill, a student at Kent State who had taken part in the Wildwood Studio project, even helped the owners, Steve and Maureen Horn, design it.

In May 2001, the owners of the Newport Motel, at Rio Grande and Ocean Avenues in Wildwood, decided to open a Subway sandwich franchise next door. At the urging of Jack Morey, the owners got permission from the Subway chain's corporate headquarters to alter the standardized design of the franchise's sign. ABS Signs was called in to create a Doo Wop sign of neon and geometric shapes, making the Wildwood Subway the first—and so far the only—Neo–Doo Wop Subway in the country.

The next Neo–Doo Wop establishment to open in The Wildwoods, in the spring of 2002, was Cool Scoops Ice Cream Parlor, at 11th and New Jersey Avenues in North Wildwood. The owner, Paul Russo, had the inside of the building designed to look just like a 1950s ice cream parlor, complete with old signs, photographs, and other assorted authentic memorabilia. Some of the booths were even shaped exactly like the back end of a '57 Chevy.

In May 2002, the long-awaited new Wildwoods Convention Center was opened to the public. Located on the ocean side of the Wildwood Boardwalk at Burk Avenue, the center was three times larger than the former

The Wildwoods' huge new Doo Wop Convention Center at Burk Avenue and the Boardwalk opened in May 2002, replacing the much smaller convention hall that had been located just across the Boardwalk. Al Alven

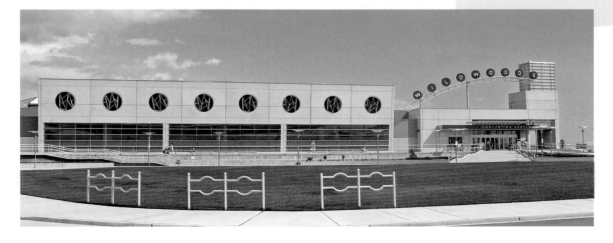

convention center which had resided in the same block on the land side of the Boardwalk since the early 1970s. With its 1950s Space Age design, neon windows, and geometric angles, the new convention center looked like something Morris Lapidus would be proud of.

In April 2003, Wildwood gained its own oldies radio station, WWZK-FM, 94.3, inside the Coastal Broadcasting Plaza located downtown at 3208 Pacific Avenue. Erik Statzell, a graphic artist with ABS Sign Company, redesigned the entire front façade of an old variety store that had once existed at that location, turning it into a modern Art Deco masterpiece with large aluminum panels and lots of neon. Oldies 94, the resident radio station, changed its call letters a year or so later to WILW-FM in honor of its hometown, to which it still refers on the air as both "the Doo Wop capital of the world" and "the birthplace of rock and roll."

On April 23, Wildwood celebrated the opening of the first Harley-Davidson franchise in The Wildwoods, on East Rio Grande Avenue in Wildwood. The new building was built to resemble an old-fashioned Art Deco style movie theater, complete with a neon marquee out front and various

The Harley-Davidson building on Rio Grande Avenue in Wildwood opened in April 2003 and is a good example of Wildwood's twenty-first-century Neo-Doo Wop architecture. Kyle Weaver

aluminum highlights in vintage 1950s style. In May, the Wawa convenience store that had been on West Rio Grande Avenue celebrated its grand reopening after being enlarged and undergoing a complete renovation. With the encouragement of Jack Morey and the Doo Wop Preservation League, it became the first Doo Wop Wawa in the country, with aluminum support posts, retro-style neon signage, and a huge angled roof over its five gas pumps.

That same spring also saw the opening of the Star Diner on New Jersey Avenue in North Wildwood. Designed around a number of interesting geometric shapes, part of the building featured green stucco walls, large flat aluminum panels, and outsize plate glass windows. Neon signage with retro 1950s-style lettering completed the unique-looking structure.

The following spring, 2004, saw the opening of the Doo Wop Diner at 4010 Boardwalk in Wildwood. Its large neon sign invited patrons into its authentic 1950s interior, which featured waitresses dressed in white blouses, saddle shoes, and poodle skirts. It all looked like something straight out of the movie *American Graffiti.*

Wildwood's Doo Wop Wawa, the only one of its kind, on Rio Grande Avenue, the main highway into The Wildwoods. A chain convenience store, it was redesigned in spring 2003 to conform to the Neo-Doo Wop building style, after encouragement from Jack Morey of the Doo Wop Preservation League.

The owners of the Subway on Rio Grande Avenue in Wildwood got permission from Subway Corporation to create a Neo-Doo Wop sign.
Kyle Weaver

The Neo–Doo Wop movement in The Wildwoods continued during 2005, as the new Commerce Bank branch office on East Rio Grande Avenue added a huge retro-style neon sign to its facility, and the local McDonald's franchise just down the block completely renovated its interior to reflect a mid-century look, adding neon highlights and various 1950s-era photos and advertisements to the interior walls. The Pink Cadillac Diner opened on Atlantic Avenue in Wildwood too, featuring a retro-1950s interior and waitresses dressed in poodle skirts like the Doo Wop Diner on the Boardwalk.

During the summer of 2005, the Shalimar Resort Motel reopened on Atlantic Avenue in Wildwood Crest. Owners Aldo and Marie Tenaglia had decided the previous year to follow Jack Morey's example with the Starlux, so they hired architect Richard Stokes to redesign their original 1964 motel into a much larger Doo Wop style facility, but with three-bedroom suites, an elevator, whirlpool baths, saunas, a large meeting room, a fitness center, and all the latest twenty-first-century amenities.

On May 25, 2006, a new Acme Market opened on Park Boulevard in Wildwood, between Hildreth and Bennett Avenues. But this was no ordinary Acme—it was widely advertised as the world's first Doo Wop Acme. The original supermarket, at the same location, had been built in 1956 and had gotten tired, outdated, and seriously worn out over its almost fifty years of existence. In the spring of 2006, it was replaced with a brand new Neo–Doo Wop facility, twice the size of the original store and sporting angled roofs and a retro neon sign with the supermarket chain's original 1950s logo on it.

No doubt about it: Neo–Doo Wop had become a permanent fixture on the landscape of The Wildwoods.

By the summer of 2006, more than a third of Wildwood's 300-plus mid-century motels had been demolished, including many of its classic Doo Wop landmarks. Despite the proliferation of Neo–Doo Wop structures in recent years, many Wildwood residents are greatly concerned not only that their island is rapidly losing its character, but also that its massive loss of motel rooms is beginning to threaten its future as a tourist resort. Though South Beach in Florida has managed to preserve its world-famous Art Deco building district from destruction in recent years, and even turned it into a hip, moneymaking asset, Wildwood has not been nearly as successful in saving its wealth of mid-century motels.

Some officials in Wildwood think the solution to losing so many motel rooms is to build twelve- to twenty-six-story-high full-service skyscrapers—decorated in the Doo Wop style—with both condo units for permanent residents

The neon sign for the Doo Wop Diner, opened in the spring of 2004 on the Wildwood Boardwalk. Kyle Weaver

The Commerce Bank
Neo-Doo Wop sign.
Kyle Weaver

and motel facilities for seasonal tourists. Others feel that such buildings would spoil the small-town charm of Wildwood and that the island's infrastructure cannot support buildings of such huge size.

"It would be a boost if the island's motels were celebrated rather than viewed as relics from a bygone era," said Jim Yost, who once managed a number of motels in Wildwood. "We've never really taken pride in our heritage. The fifties were a boom time for America, and the values were family values. It's important to play on that."

With this end in mind, the Doo Wop Preservation League released a paperback book called *How to Doo Wop* in November 2004. The purpose of the book, written by three professional architects, is to encourage owners of local mid-century buildings to hold on to those properties. It gives suggestions on how to renovate and enlarge existing buildings while preserving—and even enhancing—their mid-century Doo Wop appearance. Sales of the book so far have been moderately brisk, but whether it will help save some of Wildwood's older buildings from destruction still remains to be seen.

During the early months of 2006, some newly constructed condo buildings on the island were already in danger of being foreclosed on because they had not found buyers. The real estate boom of the early twenty-first century finally seems to be slowing down. When it eventually comes to an end, who knows what the final outcome will be? Only time will tell.

DOO WOP TIMELINE

1925

● April 11: Lewis J. Morey Sr. born in West Wildwood

1927

● September 8: Wilbert C. Morey Sr. born in West Wildwood

1945

● August 14: VJ Day; end of World War II

1946

● Beginning of baby boom generation

1948

● *Tales of the South Pacific* by James Michener is published

1949

● Googie's, a coffee shop in Los Angeles designed by architect John Lautner, opens

1950

● Morey Brothers Builders first formed, by Will and Lou Morey
● *The Kon-Tiki Expedition* by Norwegian zoologist Thor Heyerdahl is published in America

1952

- Jay's Motel, built by Morey Brothers Builders, opens in Wildwood, the first motel on the island
- First McDonald's with golden arches opens in San Bernardino, California, designed by architect Stanley Clark Meston
- Sands Hotel and Casino opens in Las Vegas, designed by Wayne McAllister
- Term "Googie architecture" is first coined by professor Douglas Haskell of Yale University in *House and Home* magazine

1953

- Summer: Bill Haley and His Comets perform at the Hof Brau Hotel in Wildwood
- Eileen Motel opens in Wildwood Crest, the first motel there
- First Denny's Coffee Shop opens in Lakewood, California, designed by architects Louis Armet and Eldon Davis, an example of Coffee Shop Modern architecture

1954

- Summer: Bill Haley and His Comets first perform "Rock around the Clock" at the Hof Brau Hotel in Wildwood
- Breezy Corner Motel opens in Wildwood Crest
- Fontainebleu Hotel opens in Miami Beach, Florida, designed by architect Morris Lapidus

1955

- Eden Roc Hotel opens in Miami Beach, Florida, designed by Morris Lapidus
- Split-level houses first introduced
- May: "Rock around the Clock" is released nationally by Bill Haley and His Comets
- Ace Sign Company opens in Wildwood, owned by Charles Caesar
- *Aku Aku* by Thor Heyerdahl is published
- Garden State Parkway opens
- Disneyland opens in Anaheim, California
- December 31: Will and Lou Morey dissolve their building partnership

1956

- March: Elvis Presley breaks into the pop music scene with "Heartbreak Hotel"
- Plymouth introduces tail fins on cars
- Hunt's Pier constructed from ruins of burned-out Hunt's Ocean Pier
- Americana Hotel opens in Miami Beach, Florida, designed by Morris Lapidus
- "Doo Wop" first attributed to the Turbans (lead singer Al Banks), a one-hit wonder rhythm-and-blue quartet from Philadelphia, with the song "When You Dance"
- April 29: Twenty-one-unit Fantasy Motel opens in Wildwood, built by Will Morey for $125,000
- Spring: Beach Waves Motel opens in Wildwood Crest
- Spring: Packard Motel opens in North Wildwood
- May 2: Dedication of Wildwood Tourism Bureau
- May 24: Schumann's Restaurant opens in Wildwood Crest, built by Will Morey
- May 27: Wildwood Diner opens in Wildwood, manufactured by Superior Diners of Berlin, New Jersey
- June: Carousel Motel opens in Wildwood Crest, built by Johnson Brothers Builders

The Ebb Tide Motel's leaning walls. MAC Collection

An early brochure drawing of the Markay Motel, located next to the Ebb Tide Motel on Atlantic Avenue in Wildwood Crest. Both motels were built at the same time, in 1957. The Markay was later renamed the Island Time Motel.
Wildwood Historical Society

The Swan Motel, built in 1958 by Lou Morey on Stockton Road in Wildwood Crest's motel district, was located right next to the Crest's spectacular beach.

1957

- Aladdin Color founded by David Bard, a local photographer who through the years will take shots of Wildwood's motels for postcards and motel brochures
- Spring: Ebb Tide Motel opens, built in Wildwood Crest by Morey Brothers Builders
- Spring: Markay Motel opens in Wildwood Crest
- Spring: Bel Air Motel opens in Wildwood Crest
- Spring: Sands Motel opens in Wildwood Crest, built by Buckingham Brothers Builders
- May 24: Jones Boys Motel opens in Wildwood, built by Lou Morey
- May 31: Eden Roc Motel opens in Wildwood, built by Lou Morey
- June 20: Town & Country Motel opens in Wildwood Crest, built by Bada Brothers Builders
- June 21: Hunt's Pier opens on Wildwood Boardwalk
- August 5: First national televised broadcast of *American Bandstand* with Dick Clark on ABC from the Starlight Ballroom on the Wildwood Boardwalk
- October 4: Sputnik launched by Russia, ushering in the Space Age

The Bel Air Motel's pool area and rooftop neon sign, made to resemble the popular 1950s automobile the motel was named after. Kyle Weaver

1958

- February: Tourist Information Center opens on Wildwood Boardwalk
- March 19: *South Pacific*, a film based on James Michener's book, is released
- Spring: Rio Motel opens in Wildwood, built by Ben Schlenzig
- Spring: Sand Castle Motel opens in Wildwood Crest
- Spring: Swan Motel opens in Wildwood Crest, built by Lou Morey
- May 17: Satellite Motel opens in Wildwood Crest, built by Will Morey
- June 1: El-Reno Motel opens in Wildwood Crest, built by Lou Morey
- June 6: Caribbean Motel opens in Wildwood Crest, built by Lou Morey
- June 14: Tangiers Motel opens in Wildwood Crest, built by Lou Morey

An early brochure illustration for the Rio Motel, showing how the original building looked in the late 1950s, before later additions.
Wildwood Historical Society

Poolside fun at the Carribbean. Kyle Weaver

The retro neon signage over the entrance to the Jolly Roger Motel.

The Beach Colony Motel, at Stockton Road and Ocean Avenue in Wildwood Crest's motel district, was built in the early 1960s.

1959

- Spring: Jolly Roger Motel opens in Wildwood Crest, built by Morey Brothers Builders
- May: Swan Motel opens in Wildwood Crest
- May: Casa Bahama Motel opens in Wildwood Crest, built by Mike Branca
- June 26: Martinique Motel opens in Wildwood
- August 21: Hawaii becomes the fiftieth state of the United States
- October 7: *Hawaiian Eye* premieres on ABC and runs until September 10, 1963

1960

- Spring: Siesta Motel opens in Wildwood Crest
- Spring: Saratoga Inn opens in Wildwood Crest
- July: Chubby Checker first introduces "The Twist" at the Rainbow Club in Wildwood
- August: "The Twist" enters music charts and becomes a national phenomenon
- October 17: Jack Morey born

1961

- May: Golden Nugget Motel opens in Wildwood Crest, built by Reno Regalbuto

1962

- March 6–8: Ash Wednesday Nor'easter hits South Jersey coast
- June 9: Nomad Motel opens in Wildwood Crest, built by Lou Morey
- June 21: All Star Motel opens in Wildwood Crest, built by Buckingham Brothers Builders
- June 24: Flagship Motel opens in Wildwood Crest, built by Will Morey
- July 1: Shore Plaza Motel opens on Wildwood Boardwalk, built by Will Morey
- July 8: Astronaut Motel opens in Wildwood Crest, built by Lou Morey
- July 8: Cara Mara Motel opens in Wildwood Crest, built by Lou Morey
- September 23: *The Jetsons* premieres on ABC and runs until September 8, 1963

1963

- George F. Boyer Historical Museum founded, located in Wildwood City Hall
- Spring: Tahiti Motel opens in Wildwood Crest
- June 15: Atlantic Diner opens in Wildwood
- June: Thunderbird Inn opens in North Wildwood
- July 4: SurfSide Restaurant opens in Wildwood Crest
- July 12: Crestwood Diner opens in Wildwood
- June: Bobby Rydell's hit "Wildwood Days" is released nationally on Cameo Records

The Astronaut Motel, part of the large complex of motels in Wildwood Crest, and its kidney-shaped pool.
Kyle Weaver

- August: "Martian Hop" released nationally on Chairman Records, recorded by the Ran-Dells, made up of Wildwood natives Steven Rappaport, Robert Rappaport, and John Spirt
- August 22: The Ran-Dells perform "Martian Hop" on *American Bandstand* on ABC
- Last year of baby boom generation

1964

- February 9: The Beatles first appear on *The Ed Sullivan Show* on CBS
- February 11: ABS Sign Company opens in Wildwood, owned by W. Robert Hentges
- April 22: New York World's Fair opens
- Spring: Red Horse Motel opens in Wildwood Crest, built by Buckingham Brothers Builders
- Spring: Admiral Motel opens in Wildwood Crest, built by Lou Morey
- Spring: Imperial 500 Motel opens in Wildwood Crest
- Spring: Shalimar Motel opens in Wildwood Crest
- Spring: Singapore Motel opens in Wildwood Crest, built by Lou Morey
- May 23: Pan American Motel opens in Wildwood Crest, built by Will Morey
- June 26: Surfrider Motel opens in North Wildwood, built by Roach Brothers Builders

1965

- October 17: New York World's Fair closes

1966

- Spring: Yankee Clipper Motel opens in Wildwood Crest, built by Lou Morey

1967

- April 15: Mid-Town Motel opens in Wildwood, built by Don Twist

1968

- Spring: Crusader Motel opens in Wildwood Crest, built by John DeFrancesco
- Spring: Olympic Motor Inn opens in Wildwood Crest, built by Lou Morey

The distinctive butterfly roof design of the Imperial 500 Motel.

1969

- Will and Bill Morey begin Boardwalk ventures by buying old Surfside Pier in North Wildwood
- Spring: Eastern section of Royal Hawaiian Motel opens in Wildwood Crest, built by Lou Morey
- Spring: Waikiki Motel opens in Wildwood Crest, built by Lou Morey

1975

- Spring: Pink Panther Motel opens in Wildwood Crest

1977

- Society for Commercial Archeology is incorporated in Vermont
- Spring: Sea Scape Inn opens in Wildwood Crest, built by Lou Morey

1978

- Will and Bill Morey buy Marine Pier on Wildwood Boardwalk and rename it Mariner's Landing Pier
- Spring: Western section of Royal Hawaiian Motel opens in Wildwood Crest, built by Lou Morey

1982

- December: B. Michael Zuckerman becomes executive director of the Mid-Atlantic Center for the Arts (MAC)

1983

- April 25: Lou Morey Sr. dies at age 58
- June: Society for Commercial Archeology meets in Wildwood and writes *Wildwood Workbook*, about Wildwood's 1950s–60s architecture

1985

- *Googie* by Alan Hess is published

1986

- Hunt's Pier sold by Bud Hunt
- The Moreys build Seapointe Village in Diamond Beach
- *Populuxe* by Thomas Hine is published

The Sea Scape Inn, built by Lou Morey in 1977 on Crocus Road in Wildwood Crest. It was one of his later motel creations.

1987

● Holly Beach Station Mall opens on Pacific Avenue in Wildwood

1991

● June 28: First '50s Doo Wop Trolley Tour in Wildwood, sponsored by MAC; brainchild of Chuck Schumann, Jack Morey, Michael Zuckerman, and Elan Zingman-Leith
● Guy F. Muziani Wildwoods Welcome Center opens at Rio Grande Avenue entrance to Wildwood
● September 7–8: First '50's Weekend held in Wildwood

1992

● Summer: Historic American Buildings Survey (HABS) study done of the Caribbean Motel in Wildwood Crest, by Alison Isenberg of the University of Pennsylvania

1993

● Midsummer: Doo Wop Trolley Tour discontinued
● Greater Wildwoods Tourism, Improvement and Development Authority (GWTIDA) formed

1995

● Doo Wop Preservation League first formed by Jack Morey and Chuck Schumann

1996

- Georgeanna Motel sold to Peter Ferriero
- April 28: Michael Zuckerman presents a slide show, "Doo Wop Architecture in The Wildwoods: Recognizing and Appreciating the Commercialuxe Styles of the 1950s and '60s," at the Common Ground Coffee House and Art Gallery, 4507 Pacific Avenue in Wildwood, sponsored by the Greater Wildwood Jaycees
- June 6: Memory Motel, formerly Georgeanna Motel, opened after $125,000 renovation
- Architect Morris Lapidus publishes his autobiography, *Too Much Is Not Enough*

1997

- February: Kent State University Architecture School students visit Wildwood to document town for the Library of Congress as an architectural treasure trove of mid-century buildings constructed between 1955 and 1965; Richard Stokes associated with these students, led by Kent State architecture professor Daniel Vieyra and University of Pennsylvania Architectural School professor Steven Izenour, a Yale University graduate and member of Venturi, Scott Brown and Associates since 1969 (Izenour previously studied the architecture of Las Vegas (1968) and Atlantic City)
- May: Nine architectural drawings done of the Caribbean Motel in Wildwood Crest by Kent State University students Timothy Wagner, Laura West, and Donna Zariczny
- September: Students from the University of Pennsylvania Graduate School of Fine Arts visit Wildwood to study architecture, led by professor and architectural historian George Thomas, Steven Izenour, and Susan Snyder; this and Kent State study sponsored by Morey Organization for $15,000
- Doo Wop Preservation League incorporated, with Jack Morey, Michael Zuckerman, Chuck Schumann, Clark Doran, Jay Ford, Ron Nardi, Steven Izenour, Elan Zingman-Leith, and Dan Vieyra on initial board
- September 18–21: Kent State University architecture professor Dan Vieyra brings the Society for Commercial Archeology to Wildwood for its Twentieth Anniversary Annual Conference; besides Vieyra, speakers include Steven Izenour, Alan Hess, and Thomas Hine

1998

- January 16: The Wildwood Studio, consisting of Kent State and University of Pennsylvania students, presents the results of its research to the public for the first time at Doo Wop Preservation League headquarters, at Pine and Pacific Avenues in Wildwood, and invites input from locals
- January 22: Will Morey Sr. dies at age 70
- Morey Organization buys Hunt's Pier on Wildwood Boardwalk
- Spring: Students from Yale School of Architecture in Wildwood to study architecture as part of an urban design study led by Steven Izenour; sponsored by the Wildwood Convention and Business Bureau for $15,000
- May 12–13: "Learning from The Wildwoods," which Izenour helped write, presented to public at Doo Wop Preservation League headquarters in Wildwood
- Spring: Doo Wop Trolley Tour restarted in Wildwood, sponsored by MAC

1999

- Robert Venturi, Denise Scott Brown, and Steven Izenour in Wildwood
- Kent State student Michael Hill helps design the Maureen Restaurant in Wildwood
- Richard Stokes (now independent) of Stokes Architecture in Philadelphia designs the Starlux Motel for Jack Morey, a $1.1 million renovation of the Wingate Motel, built in 1953
- October 11: William C. Bolger of the National Park Service holds conference in Philadelphia on "Preserving the Recent Past"

2000

- Maureen Restaurant and Martini Bar opens in Wildwood
- July: Steven Izenour asks eight more Kent State students to work in Wildwood to help preserve buildings
- "The 10 Commandments for Creating a Great Doo Wop Inspired Motel" drafted by the Wildwood Studio and Doo Wop Preservation League

- July 15: The thirty-six-unit Starlux Motel opens, funded by Jack Morey and Palmer Way family; Gov. Christine Todd Whitman dedicates the motel and "plants" a plastic palm tree in the pool area
- *The Book of Tiki: The Cult of Polynesian Pop in Fifties America* by Sven Kirsten is published
- Late: Memory Motel sold to condo developer
- November: The Doo Wop Museum at 3201 Pacific Avenue in Wildwood opens

2001

- January 18: Architect Morris Lapidus dies at age ninety-eight
- May: Subway opens; "Doo Wopped" sign made by ABS Signs for owners of the Newport Motel next door
- May: Refurbished Pizza Hut with Doo Wop sign opens
- Summer: Study begun by Nancy L. Zerbe and ARCH[2] Inc. for National Register of Historic Places designation for motel district in Wildwood Crest; Stephanie M. Hoagland of Columbia University conducts survey fieldwork
- August 22: Steven Izenour (born in 1940) dies
- Fall: Memory Motel closes for good and is demolished shortly thereafter

2002

- Spring: Two Airstream trailers arrive at Starlux Motel
- Pacific Avenue Mall in Wildwood converted back into a street
- Cool Scoops Ice Cream Parlor opens in North Wildwood
- May: The $68 million Wildwoods Convention Center opens
- Fall: Motel demolitions begin in The Wildwoods
- October 17: SurfSide Restaurant dismantled
- October: Frontier Motel in Wildwood Crest demolished
- October: Tempo Motel in Wildwood Crest demolished
- October: Sun-N-Sand Motel in North Wildwood demolished
- November: Gaslite Motel in Wildwood demolished

The SurfSide Restaurant.

2003

- April: Coastal Broadcasting Center opens on Pacific Avenue in Wildwood
- April 23: Harley-Davidson opens in Wildwood
- Spring: Schumann's Restaurant in Wildwood Crest demolished
- May: Star Diner opens in North Wildwood
- May: Refurbished Doo Wop Wawa opens on Rio Grande Avenue in Wildwood
- September 17: The 1959 Chateau Bleu Motel, at 9th and Surf Avenues in North Wildwood, placed on State Register of Historic Places
- December 1: The Doo Wop Preservation League debuts its new website at www.doowopusa.org
- December 15: Ebb Tide Motel in Wildwood Crest demolished
- December: Markay Motel (Island Time Motel) in Wildwood Crest demolished

2004

- Dan MacElrevey takes over as president of Doo Wop Preservation League from Jack Morey
- Spring: Casa Nova Motel in Wildwood Crest demolished
- Spring: Sea Rose Motel in North Wildwood demolished
- Spring: Three Coins Motel in Wildwood Crest demolished
- April: Crest Motel in Wildwood Crest demolished
- April: Town & Country Motel in Wildwood Crest demolished
- June 4: *Wildwood Days* documentary by Carolyn Travis released
- Doo Wop Diner opens on Wildwood Boardwalk
- June: Jay's Motel in Wildwood demolished
- July: Caribbean Motel sold to George Miller, Carolyn Emigh, and Mike Clark
- October: Satellite Motel in Wildwood Crest demolished
- November: *How To Doo Wop* book released by the Doo Wop Preservation League
- December: Carousel Motel in Wildwood Crest demolished
- December: Tahiti Motel in Wildwood Crest demolished

The Pink Cadillac Diner.
Kyle Weaver

2005

- February: Casa Bahama Motel in Wildwood Crest demolished
- Spring: Pink Cadillac Diner, formerly Big Ernie's Diner and the Atlantic Diner, opens in Wildwood
- April: Fantasy Motel in Wildwood demolished
- May: New Doo Wop Commerce Bank opens on Rio Grande Avenue in Wildwood
- May 4: McDonald's on Rio Grande Avenue in Wildwood unveils its new Doo Wop makeover at a ribbon-cutting ceremony
- May 6–8: Grand reopening of Caribbean Motel in Wildwood Crest
- May: Palm Beach Motel in Wildwood Crest demolished
- May: Sands Motel in Wildwood Crest demolished
- June: Swan Motel in Wildwood Crest demolished
- Summer: Breezy Corner Motel in Wildwood Crest demolished
- Summer: Monta Cello Motel in Wildwood Crest demolished
- August: Rio Motel in Wildwood demolished
- Fall: 24th Street Motel in North Wildwood demolished

A final message from the Rio Motel before its demolition in August 2005.

2006

- January: Hialeah Motel (New Carousel Motel) in Wildwood Crest demolished
- January: Shore Theater in Wildwood demolished
- January: Kona Kai Motel in Wildwood Crest demolished
- April 17: *Doo Wop Motels of The Wildwoods,* DVD documentary by Dan Espy, becomes available to public
- April 21: Groundbreaking for rebuilding of Surfside Restaurant as future Doo Wop Museum in Wildwood
- May 25: Doo Wop Acme Market opens in Wildwood
- August: The Wildwood Diner in Wildwood demolished

FURTHER READING

Doherty, Joanna Mary. "Amusement Parks as Landscapes of Popular Culture: An Analysis of Willow Grove Park and The Wildwoods." Master's thesis, University of Pennsylvania, 1999.

Dubie, Carol, Donald Jackson, and Susan Shearer. *The Wildwood Workbook.* Washington, DC: Society for Commercial Archeology, 1983.

Francis, David W., Diane Demali Francis, and Robert J. Scully, Sr. *Wildwood by the Sea: The History of an American Resort.* Fairview Park, OH: Amusement Park Books, 1998.

Futrell, Jim. *Amusement Parks of New Jersey.* Mechanicsburg, PA: Stackpole Books, 2004.

Griffin, Cara. "Cape May and Wildwood: Preservation and Revitalization Down the New Jersey Shore." Thesis, 2000.

Hess, Alan. *Googie: Fifties Coffee Shop Architecture.* San Francisco: Chronicle Books, 1985.

Hine, Thomas. *Populuxe.* New York: MJF Books, 1986, 1999.

Hirsch, Michael L. *The Wildwoods by-the-Sea Handbook of Design Standards.* Wildwood, NJ: Doo Wop Preservation League, 2003.

Hirsch, Michael Lorin, Richard Stokes, and Anthony Bracali. *How to Doo Wop.* Wildwood, NJ: Doo Wop Preservation League, 2004.

Hoagland, Stephanie Michelle. "The Conservation of 1950s and 1960s Concrete Motels in Wildwood, New Jersey." Thesis, Columbia University, 2002.

Isenberg, Alison. "Historic American Buildings Survey (HABS): Caribbean Motel, Wildwood Crest, NJ." 15 data pages. Call number: HABS NJ, 5-WILDWC, 1. Survey number: HABS NJ-1186. Card number: NJ1486. University of Pennsylvania, 1992.

Izenour, Steven, Michael Haverland, Maria Lindenfeldar, Timothy Kearney, and Daniel Vieyra. "Learning from The Wildwoods." Pamphlet, University of Pennsylvania, Yale University, and Kent State University Schools of Architecture, 1997–98.

Kirsten, Sven A. *The Book of Tiki.* Los Angeles: Taschen, 2003.

Reut, Jennifer C. "Motels, Modernism and the American Summer Vacation in Wildwood, New Jersey." Master's thesis, University of Virginia, 2004.

Wagner, Timothy, Laura West, and Donna Zariczny. "Historic American Buildings Survey (HABS): Caribbean Motel, Wildwood Crest, NJ." 9 blueprint drawings. Call number: HABS NJ, 5-WILDWC, 1. Survey number: HABS NJ-1186. Card number: NJ1486. Kent State University, 1997.

Zerbe, Nancy L. and Stephanie Michelle Hoagland. "National Register Nomination for The Wildwoods Shore Resort Historic District." ARCH[2] Inc., 2001.

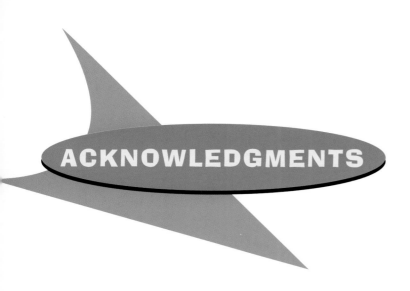

ACKNOWLEDGMENTS

I wish to express my sincere gratitude to the following individuals and organizations for their gracious help and contributions toward the content and completion of this book: Editor Kyle Weaver of Stackpole Books; David and Theresa Williams and all the members and officers of the Wildwood Crest Historical Society; Jack Morey, Lou Morey Jr., Joanne Duffy, and Joanne Galloway Rhoades of the Morey Organization; Bob Bright Jr. of the George F. Boyer (Wildwood) Historical Museum; Al Alven; B. Michael Zuckerman, Mary Stuart, and Jenn Heinold of the Mid-Atlantic Center for the Arts; Beverly Trapp of the Greater Wildwood Tourism Improvement and Development Authority; Andy Cripps of the Greater Wildwood Chamber of Commerce; Bob and Karen Cashioli of the Satellite Motel and Schumann's Restaurant; Dan MacElrevey of the Doo Wop Preservation League; Bill and Maryann Hartlein of the Casa Bahama Motel; Colleen Ahlum of the Starlux Motel; Michael Lorin Hirsch of MLH Architectural Services; Richard Stokes of Stokes Architecture; Jason W. Hesley of the Borough of Wildwood Crest; Dane Wells; Doug Hunsberger of SeaView Color; Nancy L. Zerbe of ARCH^2 Inc.; Chuck Schumann; Tony Bracali; Ed Mebs of the Greater Wildwood Hotel & Motel Association; Carolyn Travis; Stephanie Michelle Hoagland; Jennifer C. Reut; Cara Griffin; Randy Hentges of ABS Signs Inc.; W. Robert Hentges; Joe Bada Jr.; and Ed Hiller of 4 Sons Custom Palm Trees Inc. . . . Doo Wop heroes all!

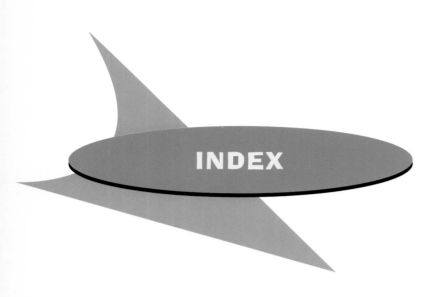

INDEX

ABOUT THE AUTHOR

Kirk Hastings grew up in Wildwood Crest, New Jersey, in the 1960s, just a few blocks away from the town's Doo Wop motel district. He has been the president of the Wildwood Crest Historical Society since 1995 and a member of the Contributing Board of the Doo Wop Preservation League since 2004. He now lives in Somers Point, just a few miles north up the Garden State Parkway from Wildwood, with his wife Sally, an elementary school teacher.